Mountain Bike
AMERICA™

G R E A T E R
BOSTON

Contact

Dear Readers:

Every effort was made to make this the most accurate, informative, and easy-to-use guidebook on the planet. Any comments, suggestions, and/or corrections regarding this guide are welcome and should be sent to:

Outside America™
c/o Editorial Dept.
300 West Main St., Ste. A
Charlottesville, VA 22903
editorial@outside-america.com
www.outside-america.com

We'd love to hear from you so we can make future editions and future guides even better.

Thanks and happy trails!

Mountain Bike™ AMERICA

GREATER BOSTON

An Atlas of the Greater Boston Area's
Greatest Off-Road Bicycle Rides
by Jeff Cutler

The Globe Pequot Press

Guilford, Connecticut

Published by
The Globe Pequot Press
P.O. Box 480
Guilford, CT 06437
www.globe-pequot.com

Produced by
Beachway Press Publishing, Inc.
300 West Main St., Ste A
Charlottesville, VA 22903
www.beachway.com

Mountain Bike America is a trademark of Beachway Press Publishing, Inc.

Editorial Assistance given by Sarah Torrey, Meredith Bosler, Lisa Gschwandtner

Cover Design Beachway Press

Photographers Jeff Cutler and Brion O'Connor

Maps designed and produced by Beachway Press

Find Outside America™ at **www.outside-america.com**

Cover Photo: A Rocky ride through Lynn Woods.

Library of Congress Cataloging-in-Publication Data is available.

ISBN 0-7627-0701-1

Manufactured in the United States of America
First Edition/First Printing

Acknowledgments

I seldom take my bike to the trails alone. This ride hasn't been any different and there were many people who rode with me or lent me support on this journey. Each helped to make compiling this book a memorable and successful project and I need to thank them.

Writers

Scott Adams' patience, direction, faith, and general good spirits made working with him and the whole Beachway team an outstanding experience. Ryan Croxton made me a better writer and made my words carry more weight. Kevin Davidsen provided me with the inspiration to keep on writing when I saw his book, *600 Days*.

Riders

Michael Bradley was my companion, trail scout, first aid station and more as he matched each of my pedal strokes on every trail in this guide. Don Gordon, John Lalone, Adam Conrad, Benji, Mary-Anne, and Dude all contributed invaluable memories as they joined me in exploring the rocks and roots throughout the Boston area. And to Phil Keyes, Bill Boles, and every NEMBA memba, you are what responsible riding is all about.

Friends

Sometimes support arrives from the most unlikely places. The many times Henry and Christian asked with genuine interest about the project made the long mapping sessions worth the work. Without Matthew, and a trip to a bike shop in 1986, I might be on a separate time line – one without bikes. And of course for Steve and all the bike shop specialists who endured my endless questions, multiple mechanicals, and special requests. You guys made it possible for me to keep riding.

Family

Mom & Dad, your encouragement allows me to succeed in everything I do. Unwavering acceptance and praise for this long-term project by Cindy, Aaron, Benji, Caroline, and Meg only reaffirm how lucky I am to have them all as siblings. And I sometimes wonder what my other parents, Susan and Charlie, first thought when I told them about this book. I never wonder about their support and belief in me.

Others

Lil, you essentially put me on my first bike. I'm sorry you're not here to enjoy this ride. And Jenna, THE BOOK is finished and you can have your dining room back. Thanks for putting up with the bikes in the house.

Table Of

Contents

Appendix

Index

Meet the Author

Preface

At age eight, I had a Big Wheel. A few years later I rode a five-speed chopper. In junior high I exchanged a red and black BMX for a red Raleigh ten-speed – trading cool for practical. Then the bikes started to fade away. I owned a car and had very little interest in getting somewhere at 14 miles an hour when I could get there at 70.

Then came college and in 1986 Matthew Manes put me back on track. We went to International Bicycle in Allston where I bought a Specialized StreetStomper for $375. Shortly thereafter I became a bike messenger in Boston. My love for the sport came back quickly and soon I was riding the steps at the Prudential, along the pool at the Christian Science Center, and over the footbridges throughout the city.

In 1995, I was still riding the StreetStomper and decided to try real mountain biking. My best friend Michael and I went to Wompatuck State Park. The mountain biking bug was like a yawn during a meeting and Michael and I were quickly infected. My quasi-knobbies were exchanged for real tires, grip shift was added, I put on bar ends, and I got rid of my riser bar. All summer, Mike and I beat on our bikes. We rode in Boston in the evenings and Wompatuck during the days. I quickly realized the limits of the StreetStomper. It was time for a new bike.

Grandma Lil helped finance a purple and green Trek 930 SHX. It was with that bike I broke my collarbone twice and landed a fantastic job writing about mountain bike trails. Lil also helped me buy a blue M2 StumpJumper frame.

Looking back, I can truly appreciate the impact biking has had, and still has, on my life. It's taught me lessons in physics and gravity, loyalty and reliability, self-sufficiency and perseverance, and managing my feelings and conquering my fears. A bike is more than transportation or recreation. It's a vehicle that can take you far away or very close to home.

There are now nine bikes in my house, I've ridden nearly everywhere in eastern Massachusetts, and I'm busy planning mountain bike trips to Moab and California. Riding has strengthened my relationships, made me a happier person, and has helped make some of my dreams come true.

I hope this book and the trails within take you to places you could only imagine—both physically and mentally. Some trails will give you permagrin and others will make you grimace, it's up to you to find out which ones. But you can only get there one way—just ride.

Introduc

A note from the folks behind this endeavor...

We at Outside America look at guidebook publishing a little differently. There's just no reason that a guidebook has to look like it was published out of your Uncle Ernie's woodshed. We feel that guidebooks need to be both easy to use and nice to look at, and that takes an innovative approach to design. You see, we want you to spend less time fumbling through your guidebook and more time enjoying the adventure at hand. At any rate, we hope you like what you see and enjoy the places we lead you. And most of all, we'd like to thank you for taking an adventure with us.

Happy Trails!

Introduction

Welcome to the new generation of bicycling! Indeed, the sport has evolved dramatically from the thin-tired, featherweight-frame days of old. The sleek geometry and lightweight frames of racing bicycles, still the heart and soul of bicycling worldwide, have lost much ground in recent years, unpaving the way for the mountain bike, which now accounts for the majority of all bicycle sales in the U.S. And with this change comes a new breed of cyclist, less concerned with smooth roads and long rides, who thrives in places once inaccessible to the mortal road bike.

The mountain bike, with its knobby tread and reinforced frame, takes cyclists to places once unheard of—down rugged mountain trails, through streams of rushing water, across the frozen Alaskan tundra, and even to work in the city. There seem to be few limits on what this fat-tired beast can do and where it can take us. Few obstacles stand in its way, few boundaries slow its progress. Except for one—its own success. If trail closure means little to you now, read on and discover how a trail can be here today and gone tomorrow. With so many new off-road cyclists taking to the trails each year, it's no wonder trail access hinges precariously between universal acceptance and complete termination. But a little work on your part can go a long way to preserving trail access for future use. Nothing is more crucial to the survival of mountain biking itself than to read the examples set forth in the following pages and practice their message. Then turn to the maps, pick out your favorite ride, and hit the dirt!

WHAT THIS BOOK IS ABOUT

Within these pages you will find everything you need to know about off-road bicycling in Boston. This guidebook begins by exploring the fascinating history of the mountain bike itself, then goes on to discuss everything from the health benefits of off-road cycling to tips and techniques for bicycling over logs and up hills. Also included are the types of clothing to keep you comfortable and in style, essential equipment ideas to keep your rides smooth and trouble-free, and descriptions of off-road terrain to prepare you for the kinds of bumps and bounces you can expect to encounter. The major provisions of this book, though, are its unique perspectives on each ride, it detailed maps, and its relentless dedication to trail preservation.

Without open trails, the maps in this book are virtually useless. Cyclists must learn to be responsible for the trails they use and to share these trails with others. This guidebook addresses such issues as why trail use has become so controversial, what can be done to improve the image of mountain biking, how to have fun and ride responsibly, on-the-spot trail repair techniques, trail maintenance hotlines for each trail, and the worldwide-standard Rules of the Trail.

Each of the 29 rides is complete with maps, photos, trail descriptions and directions, local history, and a quick-reference ride information guide including such items as trail contact information, park schedules, fees/permits, local bike stores, dining, lodging, entertainment, alternative map resources and more. It's important to note that mountain bike rides tend to take longer than road rides because the average speed is often much slower. Average speeds can vary from a climbing pace of three to four miles per hour to 12 to 13 miles per hour on flatter roads and trails. Keep this in mind when planning your trip.

MOUNTAIN BIKE BEGINNINGS

It seems the mountain bike, originally designed for lunatic adventurists bored with straight lines, clean clothes, and smooth tires, has become globally popular in as short a time as it would take to race down a mountain trail.

Like many things of a revolutionary nature, the mountain bike was born on the west coast. But unlike Rollerblades, purple hair, and the peace sign, the concept of the off-road bike cannot be credited solely to the imaginative Californians—they were just the first to make waves.

The design of the first off-road specific bike was based on the geometry of the old Schwinn Excelsior, a one-speed, camel-back cruiser with balloon tires. Joe Breeze was the creator behind it, and in 1977 he built 10 of these "Breezers" for himself and his Marin County, California, friends at $750 apiece—a bargain.

Breeze was a serious competitor in bicycle racing, placing 13th in the 1977 U.S. Road Racing National Championships. After races, he and friends would scour local bike shops hoping to find old bikes they could then restore.

It was the 1941 Schwinn Excelsior, for which Breeze paid just five dollars, that began to shape and change bicycling history forever. After taking the bike home, removing the fenders, oiling the chain, and pumping up the tires, Breeze hit the dirt. He loved it.

His inspiration, while forerunning, was not altogether unique. On the opposite end of the country, nearly 2,500 miles from Marin County, east coast bike bums were also growing restless. More and more old, beat-up clunkers were being restored and modified. These behemoths often weighed as much as 80 pounds and were so reinforced they seemed virtually indestructible. But rides that take just 40 minutes on today's 25-pound featherweights took the steel-toed-boot- and-blue-jean-clad bikers of the late 1970s and early 1980s nearly four hours to complete.

Not until 1981 was it possible to purchase a production mountain bike, but local retailers found these ungainly bicycles difficult to sell and rarely kept them in stock. By 1983, however, mountain bikes were no longer such a fringe item, and large bike manufacturers quickly jumped into the action, producing their own versions of the off-road bike. By the 1990s, the mountain bike had firmly established its place with bicyclists of nearly all ages and abilities, and now command nearly 90 percent of the U.S. bike market.

There are many reasons for the mountain bike's success in becoming the hottest two-wheeled vehicle in the nation. They are much friendlier to the cyclist than traditional road bikes because of their comfortable upright position and shock-absorbing fat tires. And because of the health-conscious, environmentalist movement of the late 1980s and 1990s, people are more activity minded and seek nature on a closer front than paved roads can allow. The mountain bike gives you these things and takes you far away from the daily grind—even if you're only minutes from the city.

MOUNTAIN BIKING INTO SHAPE

If your objective is to get in shape and lose weight, then you're on the right track, because mountain biking is one of the best ways to get started.

One way many of us have lost weight in this sport is the crash-and-burn-it-off method. Picture this: you're speeding uncontrollably down a vertical drop that you realize you shouldn't be on—only after it is too late. Your front wheel lodges into a rut and launches you through endless weeds, trees, and pointy rocks before coming to an abrupt halt in a puddle of thick mud. Surveying the damage, you discover, with the layers of skin, body parts, and lost confidence littering the trail above, that those unwanted pounds have been shed—*permanently*. Instant weight loss.

There is, of course, a more conventional (and quite a bit less painful) approach to losing weight and gaining fitness on a mountain bike. It's called the workout, and bicycles provide an ideal way to get physical. Take a look at some of the benefits associated with cycling.

Cycling helps you shed pounds without gimmicky diet fads or weight-loss programs. You can explore the countryside and burn nearly 10 to 16 calories per minute or close to 600 to 1,000 calories per hour. Moreover, it's a great way to spend an afternoon.

No less significant than the external and cosmetic changes of your body from riding are the internal changes taking place. Over time, cycling regularly will strengthen your heart as your body grows vast networks of new capillaries to carry blood to all those working muscles. This will, in turn, give your skin a healthier glow. The capacity of your lungs may increase up to 20 percent, and your resting heart rate will drop significantly. The Stanford University School of Medicine reports to the American Heart Association that people can reduce their risk of heart attack by nearly 64 percent if they can burn up to 2,000 calories per week. This is only two to three hours of bike riding!

Recommended for insomnia, hypertension, indigestion, anxiety, and even for recuperation from major heart attacks, bicycling can be an excellent cure-all as well as a great preventive. Cycling just a few hours per week can improve your figure and sleeping habits, give you greater resistance to illness, increase your energy levels, and provide feelings of accomplishment and heightened self-esteem.

BE SAFE—KNOW THE LAW

Occasionally, even the hard-core off-road cyclists will find they have no choice but to ride the pavement. When you are forced to hit the road, it's important for you to know and understand the rules.

Outlined below are a few of the common laws found in Boston's Vehicle Code book.

- *Bicycles are legally classified as vehicles in Boston.* This means that as a bicyclist, you are responsible for obeying the same rules of the road as a driver of a motor vehicle.
- *Bicyclists must ride with the traffic—NOT AGAINST IT!* Because bicycles are considered vehicles, you must ride your bicycle just as you would drive a car—with traffic. Only pedestrians should travel against the flow of traffic.

3

- *You must obey all traffic signs.* This includes stop signs and stoplights.
- *Always signal your turns.* Most drivers aren't expecting bicyclists to be on the roads, and many drivers would prefer that cyclists stay off the roads altogether. It's important, therefore, to clearly signal your intentions to motorists both in front and behind you.
- *Bicyclists are entitled to the same roads as cars (except controlled-access highways).* Unfortunately, cyclists are rarely given this consideration.
- *Be a responsible cyclist.* Do not abuse your rights to ride on open roads. Follow the rules and set a good example for all of us as you roll along.

THE MOUNTAIN BIKE CONTROVERSY

Are Off-Road Bicyclists Environmental Outlaws? Do We have the Right to Use Public Trails?
Mountain bikers have long endured the animosity of folks in the backcountry who complain about the consequences of off-road bicycling. Many people believe that the fat tires and knobby tread do unacceptable environmental damage and that our uncontrollable riding habits are a danger to animals and to other trail users. To the contrary, mountain bikes have no more environmental impact than hiking boots or horseshoes. This does not mean, however, that mountain bikes leave no imprint at all. Wherever man treads, there is an impact. By riding responsibly, though, it is possible to leave only a minimum impact—something we all must take care to achieve.

Unfortunately, it is often people of great influence who view the mountain bike as the environment's worst enemy. Consequently, we as mountain bike riders and environmentally concerned citizens must be educators, impressing upon others that we also deserve the right to use these trails. Our responsibilities as bicyclists are no more and no less than any other trail user. We must all take the soft-cycling approach and show that mountain bicyclists are not environmental outlaws.

ETIQUETTE OF MOUNTAIN BIKING

When discussing mountain biking etiquette, we are in essence discussing the soft-cycling approach. This term, as mentioned previously, describes the art of minimum-impact bicycling and should apply to both the physical and social dimensions of the sport. But make no mistake—it is possible to ride fast and furiously while maintaining the balance of soft-cycling. Here first are a few ways to minimize the physical impact of mountain bike riding.

- *Stay on the trail.* Don't ride around fallen trees or mud holes that block your path. Stop and cross over them. When you come to a vista overlooking a deep valley, don't ride off the trail for a better vantage point. Instead, leave the bike and walk to see the view. Riding off the trail may seem inconsequential when done only once, but soon someone else will follow, then others, and the cumulative results can be catastrophic. Each time you wander from the trail you begin creating a new path, adding one more scar to the earth's surface.
- *Do not disturb the soil.* Follow a line within the trail that will not disturb or damage the soil.

4

- *Do not ride over soft or wet trails.* After a rain shower or during the thawing season, trails will often resemble muddy, oozing swampland. The best thing to do is stay off the trails altogether. Realistically, however, we're all going to come across some muddy trails we cannot anticipate. Instead of blasting through each section of mud, which may seem both easier and more fun, lift the bike and walk past. Each time a cyclist rides through a soft or muddy section of trail, that part of the trail is permanently damaged. Regardless of the trail's conditions, though, remember always to go over the obstacles across the path, not around them. Stay on the trail.
- *Avoid trails that, for all but God, are considered impassable and impossible.* Don't take a leap of faith down a kamikaze descent on which you will be forced to lock your brakes and skid to the bottom, ripping the ground apart as you go.

Soft-cycling should apply to the social dimensions of the sport as well, since mountain bikers are not the only folks who use the trails. Hikers, equestrians, cross-country skiers, and other outdoors people use many of the same trails and can be easily spooked by a marauding mountain biker tearing through the trees. Be friendly in the forest and give ample warning of your approach.

- *Take out what you bring in.* Don't leave broken bike pieces and banana peels scattered along the trail.
- *Be aware of your surroundings.* Don't use popular hiking trails for race training.
- *Slow down!* Rocketing around blind corners is a sure way to ruin an unsuspecting hiker's day. Consider this—If you fly down a quick singletrack descent at 20 mph, then hit the brakes and slow down to only six mph to pass someone, you're still moving twice as fast as they are!

Like the trails we ride on, the social dimension of mountain biking is very fragile and must be cared for responsibly. We should not want to destroy another person's enjoyment of the outdoors. By riding in the backcountry with caution, control, and responsibility, our presence should be felt positively by other trail users. By adhering to these rules, trail riding—a privilege that can quickly be taken away—will continue to be ours to share.

TRAIL MAINTENANCE

Unfortunately, despite all of the preventive measures taken to avoid trail damage, we're still going to run into many trails requiring attention. Simply put, a lot of hikers, equestrians, and cyclists alike use the same trails—some wear and tear is unavoidable. But like your bike, if you want to use these trails for a long time to come, you must also maintain them.

Trail maintenance and restoration can be accomplished in a variety of ways. One way is for mountain bike clubs to combine efforts with other trail users (i.e. hikers and equestrians) and work closely with land managers to cut new trails or repair existing ones. This not only reinforces to others the commitment cyclists have in caring for and maintaining the land, but also breaks the ice that often separates cyclists from their fellow trailmates. Another good way to help out is to show up on a Saturday morning with a few riding buddies at your favorite off-road domain ready to work. With a good attitude, thick gloves, and the local land manager's supervision, trail repair is fun and very rewarding. It's important, of course, that you arrange a trail-repair outing with the local land manager before you start pounding shovels into the dirt. They can lead you to the most needy sections of trail and instruct you on what repairs should be done and how best to accomplish the task. Perhaps the most effective means of trail maintenance, though, can be done by yourself and while you're riding. Read on.

ON-THE-SPOT QUICK FIX

Most of us, when we're riding, have at one time or another come upon muddy trails or fallen trees blocking our path. We notice that over time the mud gets deeper and the trail gets wider as people go through or around the obstacles. We worry that the problem will become so severe and repairs too difficult that the trail's access may be threatened. We also know that our ambition to do anything about it is greatest at that moment, not after a hot shower and a plate of spaghetti. Here are a few on-the-spot quick fixes you can do that will hopefully correct a problem before it gets out of hand and get you back on your bike within minutes.

Muddy Trails. What do you do when trails develop huge mud holes destined for the EPA's Superfund status? The technique is called corduroying, and it works much like building a pontoon over the mud to support bikes, horses, or hikers as they cross. Corduroy (not the pants) is the term for roads made of logs laid down crosswise. Use small-and medium-sized sticks and lay them side by side across the trail until they cover the length of the muddy section (break the sticks to fit the width of the trail). Press them into the mud with your feet, then lay more on top if needed. Keep adding sticks until the trail is firm. Not only will you stay clean as you cross, but the sticks may soak up some of the water and help the puddle dry. This quick fix may last as long as one month before needing to be redone. And as time goes on, with new layers added to the trail, the soil will grow stronger, thicker, and more resistant to erosion. This whole process may take fewer than five minutes, and you can be on your way, knowing the trail behind you is in good repair.

Leaving the Trail. What do you do to keep cyclists from cutting corners and leaving the designated trail? The solution is much simpler than you may think. (No, don't hire an off-road police force.) Notice where people are leaving the trail and throw a pile of thick branches or brush along the path, or place logs across the opening to block the way through. There are probably dozens of subtle tricks like these that will manipulate people into staying on the designated trail. If executed well, no one will even notice that the thick branches scattered along the ground in the woods weren't always there. And most folks would probably rather take a moment to hop a log in the trail than get tangled in a web of branches.

Obstacle in the Way. If there are large obstacles blocking the trail, try and remove them or push them aside. If you cannot do this by yourself, call the trail maintenance hotline to speak with the land manager of that particular trail and see what can be done.

We must be willing to sweat for our trails in order to sweat on them. Police yourself and point out to others the significance of trail maintenance. "Sweat Equity," the rewards of continued land use won with a fair share of sweat, pays off when the trail is "up for review" by the land manager and he or she remembers the efforts made by trail-conscious mountain bikers.

RULES OF THE TRAIL

The International Mountain Bicycling Association (IMBA) has developed these guidelines to trail riding. These "Rules of the Trail" are accepted worldwide and will go a long way in keeping trails open. Please respect and follow these rules for everyone's sake.

1. **Ride only on open trails.** Respect trail and road closures (if you're not sure, ask a park or state official first), do not trespass on private property, and obtain permits or authorization if required. Federal and state wilderness areas are off-limits to cycling. Parks and state forests may also have certain trails closed to cycling.

2. **Leave no trace.** Be sensitive to the dirt beneath you. Even on open trails, you should not ride under conditions by which you will leave evidence of your passing, such as on certain soils or shortly after a rainfall. Be sure to observe the different types of soils and trails you're riding on, practicing minimum-impact cycling. Never ride off the trail, don't skid your tires, and be sure to bring out at least as much as you bring in.

3. **Control your bicycle!** Inattention for even one second can cause disaster for yourself or for others. Excessive speed frightens and can injure people, gives mountain biking a bad name, and can result in trail closures.

4. **Always yield.** Let others know you're coming well in advance (a friendly greeting is always good and often appreciated). Show your respect when passing others by slowing to walking speed or stopping altogether, especially in the presence of horses. Horses can be unpredictable, so be very careful. Anticipate that other trail users may be around corners or in blind spots.

5. **Never spook animals.** All animals are spooked by sudden movements, unannounced approaches, or loud noises. Give the animals extra room and time so they can adjust to you. Move slowly or dismount around animals. Running cattle and disturbing wild animals are serious offenses. Leave gates as you find them, or as marked.

6. **Plan ahead.** Know your equipment, your ability, and the area in which you are riding, and plan your trip accordingly. Be self-sufficient at all times, keep your bike in good repair, and carry necessary supplies for changes in weather or other conditions. You can help keep trails open by setting an example of responsible, courteous, and controlled mountain bike riding.

7. **Always wear a helmet when you ride.** For your own safety and protection, a helmet should be worn whenever you are riding your bike. You never know when a tree root or small rock will throw you the wrong way and send you tumbling.

Thousands of miles of dirt trails have been closed to mountain bicycling because of the irresponsible riding habits of just a few riders. Don't follow the example of these offending riders. Don't take away trail privileges from thousands of others who work hard each year to keep the backcountry avenues open to us all.

THE NECESSITIES OF CYCLING

When discussing the most important items to have on a bike ride, cyclists generally agree on the following four items.

Helmet. The reasons to wear a helmet should be obvious. Helmets are discussed in more detail in the *Be Safe—Wear Your Armor* section.

Water. Without it, cyclists may face dehydration, which may result in dizziness and fatigue. On a warm day, cyclists should drink at least one full bottle during every hour of riding. Remember, it's always good to drink before you feel thirsty—otherwise, it may be too late.

Cycling Shorts. These are necessary if you plan to ride your bike more than 20 to 30 minutes. Padded cycling shorts may be the only thing preventing your derriere from serious saddle soreness by ride's end. There are two types of cycling shorts you can buy. Touring shorts are good for people who don't want to look like they're wearing anatomically correct cellophane. These look like regular athletic shorts with pockets, but have built-in padding in the crotch area for protection from chafing and saddle sores. The more popular, traditional cycling shorts are made of skin-tight material, also with a padded crotch. Whichever style you find most comfortable, cycling shorts are a necessity for long rides.

Food. This essential item will keep you rolling. Cycling burns up a lot of calories and is among the few sports in which no one is safe from the "Bonk." Bonking feels like it sounds. Without food in your system, your blood sugar level collapses, and there is no longer any energy in your body. This instantly results in total fatigue and light-headedness. So when you're filling your water bottle, remember to bring along some food. Fruit, energy bars, or some other forms of high-energy food are highly recommended. Candy bars are not, however, because they will deliver a sudden burst of high energy, then let you down soon after, causing you to feel worse than before. Energy bars are available at most bike stores and are similar to candy bars, but provide complex carbohydrate energy and high nutrition rather than fast-burning simple sugars.

BE PREPARED OR DIE

Essential equipment that will keep you from dying alone in the woods:

- **Spare Tube**
- **Tire Irons**—See the Appendix for instructions on fixing flat tires.
- **Patch Kit**
- **Pump**
- **Money**—Spare change for emergency calls.

- **Spoke Wrench**
- **Spare Spokes**—To fit your wheel. Tape these to the chain stay.
- **Chain Tool**
- **Allen Keys**—Bring appropriate sizes to fit your bike.
- **Compass**
- **First-Aid Kit**
- **Rain Gear**—For quick changes in weather.
- **Matches**
- **Guidebook**—In case all else fails and you must start a fire to survive, this guidebook will serve as excellent fire starter!

To carry these items, you may need a bike bag. A bag mounted in front of the handlebars provides quick access to your belongings, whereas a saddle bag fitted underneath the saddle keeps things out of your way. If you're carrying lots of equipment, you may want to consider a set of panniers. These are much larger and mount on either side of each wheel on a rack. Many cyclists, though, prefer not to use a bag at all. They just slip all they need into their jersey pockets, and off they go.

BE SAFE—WEAR YOUR ARMOR

While on the subject of jerseys, it's crucial to discuss the clothing you must wear to be safe, practical, and—if you prefer—stylish. The following is a list of items that will save you from disaster, outfit you comfortably, and most important, keep you looking cool.

Helmet. A helmet is an absolute necessity because it protects your head from complete annihilation. It is the only thing that will not disintegrate into a million pieces after a wicked crash on a descent you shouldn't have been on in the first place. A helmet with a solid exterior shell will also protect your head from sharp or protruding objects. Of course, with a hard-shelled helmet, you can paste several stickers of your favorite bicycle manufacturers all over the outer shell, giving companies even more free advertising for your dollar.

Shorts. Let's just say Lycra™ cycling shorts are considered a major safety item if you plan to ride for more than 20 or 30 minutes at a time. As mentioned in *The Necessities of Cycling* section, cycling shorts are well regarded as the leading cure-all for chafing and saddle sores. The most preventive cycling shorts have padded "chamois" (most chamois is synthetic nowadays) in the crotch area. Of course, if you choose to wear these traditional cycling shorts, it's imperative that they look as if someone spray painted them onto your body.

Gloves. You may find well-padded cycling gloves invaluable when traveling over rocky trails and gravelly roads for hours on end. Long-fingered gloves may also be useful, as branches, trees, assorted hard objects, and, occasionally, small animals will reach out and whack your knuckles.

Glasses. Not only do sunglasses give you an imposing presence and make you look cool (both are extremely important), they also protect your eyes from harmful ultraviolet rays, invisible branches, creepy bugs, dirt, and may prevent you from being caught sneaking glances at riders of the opposite sex also wearing skintight, revealing Lycra™.

Shoes. Mountain bike shoes should have stiff soles to help make pedaling easier and provide better traction when walking your bike up a trail becomes necessary. Virtually any kind of good outdoor hiking footwear will work, but specific mountain bike shoes (especially those with inset cleats) are best. It is vital that these shoes look as ugly as humanly possible. Those closest in style to bowling shoes are, of course, the most popular.

Jersey or Shirt. Bicycling jerseys are popular because of their snug fit and back pockets. When purchasing a jersey, look for ones that are loaded with bright, blinding, neon logos and manufacturers' names. These loudly decorated billboards are also good for drawing unnecessary attention to yourself just before taking a mean spill while trying to hop a curb. A cotton T-shirt is a good alternative in warm weather, but when the weather turns cold, cotton becomes a chilling substitute for the jersey. Cotton retains moisture and sweat against your body, which may cause you to get the chills and ills on those cold-weather rides.

OH, THOSE COLD BOSTON DAYS

If the weather chooses not to cooperate on the day you've set aside for a bike ride, it's helpful to be prepared.

Tights or leg warmers. These are best in temperatures below 55 degrees. Knees are sensitive and can develop all kinds of problems if they get cold. Common problems include tendinitis, bursitis, and arthritis.

Plenty of layers on your upper body. When the air has a nip in it, layers of clothing will keep the chill away from your chest and help prevent the development of bronchitis. If the air is cool, a Polypropylene™ or Capilene™ long-sleeved shirt is best to wear against the skin beneath other layers of clothing. Polypropylene or Capilene, like wool, wicks away moisture from your skin to keep your body dry. Try to avoid wearing cotton or baggy clothing when the temperature falls. Cotton, as mentioned before, holds moisture like a sponge, and baggy clothing catches cold air and swirls it around your body. Good cold-weather clothing should fit snugly against your body, but not be restrictive.

Wool socks. Don't pack too many layers under those shoes, though. You may stand the chance of restricting circulation, and your feet will get real cold, real fast.

Thinsulate or Gortex™ gloves. We may all agree that there is nothing worse than frozen feet—unless your hands are frozen. A good pair of Thinsulate™ or Gortex™ gloves should keep your hands toasty and warm.

Hat or helmet on cold days? Sometimes, when the weather gets really cold and you still want to hit the trails, it's tough to stay warm. We all know that 130 percent of the body's heat escapes through the head (overactive brains, I imagine), so it's important to keep the cranium warm. Ventilated helmets are designed to keep heads cool in the summer heat, but they do little to help keep heads warm during rides in sub-zero temperatures. Cyclists should consider wearing a hat on extremely cold days.

Capilene Skullcaps are great head and ear warmers that snugly fit over your head beneath the helmet. Head protection is not lost. Another option is a helmet cover that covers those ventilating gaps and helps keep the body heat in. These do not, however, keep your ears warm. Some cyclists will opt for a simple knit cycling cap sans the helmet, but these have never been shown to be very good cranium protectors.

All of this clothing can be found at your local bike store, where the staff should be happy to help fit you into the seasons of the year.

TO HAVE OR NOT TO HAVE... *(Other Very Useful Items)*

Though mountain biking is relatively new to the cycling scene, there is no shortage of items for you and your bike to make riding better, safer, and easier. We have rummaged through the unending lists and separated the gadgets from the good stuff, coming up with what we believe are items certain to make mountain bike riding easier and more enjoyable.

Tires. Buying yourself a good pair of knobby tires is the quickest way to enhance the off-road handling capabilities of your bike. There are many types of mountain bike tires on the market. Some are made exclusively for very rugged off-road terrain. These big-knobbed, soft rubber tires virtually stick to the ground with unforgiving traction, but tend to deteriorate quickly on pavement. There are other tires made exclusively for the road. These are called "slicks" and have no tread at all. For the average cyclist, though, a good tire somewhere in the middle of these two extremes should do the trick.

Toe Clips or Clipless Pedals. With these, you will ride with more power. Toe clips attach to your pedals and strap your feet firmly in place, allowing you to exert pressure on the pedals on both the downstroke and the upstroke. They will increase your pedaling efficiency by 30 percent to 50 percent. Clipless pedals, which liberate your feet from the traditional straps and clips, have made toe clips virtually obsolete. Like ski bindings, they attach your shoe directly to the pedal. They are, however, much more expensive than toe clips.

Bar Ends. These great clamp-on additions to your original straight bar will provide more leverage, an excellent grip for climbing, and a more natural position for your hands. Be aware, however, of the bar end's propensity for hooking trees on fast descents, sending you, the cyclist, airborne.

Fanny Pack. These bags are ideal for carrying keys, extra food, guidebooks, tools, spare tubes, and a cellular phone, in case you need to call for help.

Suspension Forks. For the more serious off-roaders who want nothing to impede their speed on the trails, investing in a pair of suspension forks is a good idea. Like tires, there are plenty of brands to choose from, and they all do the same thing—absorb the brutal beatings of a rough trail. The cost of these forks, however, is sometimes more brutal than the trail itself.

Bike Computers. These are fun gadgets to own and are much less expensive than in years past. They have such features as trip distance, speedometer, odometer, time of day, altitude, alarm, average speed, maximum speed, heart rate, global satellite positioning, etc. Bike computers will come in handy when following these maps or to know just how far you've ridden in the wrong direction.

Water Pack. This is quickly becoming an essential item for cyclists pedaling for more than a few hours, especially in hot, dry conditions. The most popular brand is, of course, the Camelback™, and these water packs can carry in their bladder bags as much as 100 ounces of water. These packs strap onto your back with a handy hose running over your shoulder so you can be drinking water while still holding onto the bars on a rocky descent with both hands. These packs are a great way to carry a lot of extra liquid on hot rides in the middle of nowhere.

TYPES OF OFF-ROAD TERRAIN

Before roughing it off road, we may first have to ride the pavement to get to our destination. Please, don't be dismayed. Some of the country's best rides are on the road. Once we get past these smooth-surfaced pathways, though, adventures in dirt await us.

Rails-to-Trails. Abandoned rail lines are converted into usable public resources for exercising, commuting, or just enjoying nature. Old rails and ties are torn up and a trail, paved or unpaved, is laid along the existing corridor. This completes the cycle from ancient Indian trading routes to railroad corridors and back again to hiking and cycling trails.

Unpaved Roads are typically found in rural areas and are most often public roads. Be careful when exploring, though, not to ride on someone's unpaved private drive.

Forest Roads. These dirt and gravel roads are used primarily as access to forest land and are generally kept in good condition. They are almost always open to public use.

Singletrack can be the most fun on a mountain bike. These trails, with only one track to follow, are often narrow, challenging pathways through the woods. Remember to make sure these trails are open before zipping into the woods. (At the time of this printing, all trails and roads in this guidebook were open to mountain bikes.)

Open Land. Unless there is a marked trail through a field or open space, you should not plan to ride here. Once one person cuts his or her wheels through a field or meadow, many more are sure to follow, causing irreparable damage to the landscape.

TECHNIQUES TO SHARPEN YOUR SKILLS

Many of us see ourselves as pure athletes—blessed with power, strength, and endless endurance. However, it may be those with finesse, balance, agility, and grace that get around most quickly on a mountain bike. Although power, strength, and endurance do have their places in mountain biking, these elements don't necessarily form the framework for a champion mountain biker.

The bike should become an extension of your body. Slight shifts in your hips or knees can have remarkable results. Experienced bike handlers seem to flash down technical descents, dashing over obstacles in a smooth and graceful effort as if pirouetting in Swan

Lake. Here are some tips and techniques to help you connect with your bike and float gracefully over the dirt.

Braking

Using your brakes requires using your head, especially when descending. This doesn't mean using your head as a stopping block, but rather to think intelligently. Use your best judgment in terms of how much or how little to squeeze those brake levers.

The more weight a tire is carrying, the more braking power it has. When you're going downhill, your front wheel carries more weight than the rear. Braking with the front brake will help keep you in control without going into a skid. Be careful, though, not to overdo it with the front brakes and accidentally toss yourself over the handlebars. And don't neglect your rear brake! When descending, shift your weight back over the rear wheel, thus increasing your rear braking power as well. This will balance the power of both brakes and give you maximum control.

Good riders learn just how much of their weight to shift over each wheel and how to apply just enough braking power to each brake, so not to "endo" over the handlebars or skid down a trail.

GOING UPHILL—*Climbing Those Treacherous Hills*

Shift into a low gear (push the shifter away from you). Before shifting, be sure to ease up on your pedaling so there is not too much pressure on the chain. Find the gear best for you that matches the terrain and steepness of each climb.
Stay seated. Standing out of the saddle is often helpful when climbing steep hills with a road bike, but you may find that on dirt, standing may cause your rear tire to lose its grip and spin out. Climbing requires traction. Stay seated as long as you can, and keep the rear tire digging into the ground. Ascending skyward may prove to be much easier in the saddle.
Lean forward. On very steep hills, the front end may feel unweighted and suddenly pop up. Slide forward on the saddle and lean over the handlebars. This will add more weight to the front wheel and should keep you grounded.
Keep pedaling. On rocky climbs, be sure to keep the pressure on, and don't let up on those pedals! The slower you go through rough trail sections, the harder you will work.

GOING DOWNHILL—*The Real Reason We Get Up in the Morning*

Shifting into the big chainring before a bumpy descent will help keep the chain from bouncing off. And should you crash or disengage your leg from the pedal, the chain will cover the teeth of the big ring so they don't bite into your leg.
Relax. Stay loose on the bike, and don't lock your elbows or clench your grip. Your elbows need to bend with the bumps and absorb the shock, while your hands should have a firm but controlled grip on the bars to keep things steady. Steer with

your body, allowing your shoulders to guide you through each turn and around each obstacle.

Don't oversteer or lose control. Mountain biking is much like downhill skiing, since you must shift your weight from side to side down narrow, bumpy descents. Your bike will have the tendency to track in the direction you look and follow the slight shifts and leans of your body. You should not think so much about steering, but rather in what direction you wish to go.

Rise above the saddle. When racing down bumpy, technical descents, you should not be sitting on the saddle, but standing on the pedals, allowing your legs and knees to absorb the rocky trail instead of your rear.

Drop your saddle. For steep, technical descents, you may want to drop your saddle three or four inches. This lowers your center of gravity, giving you much more room to bounce around.

Keep your pedals parallel to the ground. The front pedal should be slightly higher so that it doesn't catch on small rocks or logs.

Stay focused. Many descents require your utmost concentration and focus just to reach the bottom. You must notice every groove, every root, every rock, every hole, every bump. You, the bike, and the trail should all become one as you seek singletrack nirvana on your way down the mountain. But if your thoughts wander, however, then so may your bike, and you may instead become one with the trees!

WATCH OUT!
Back-road Obstacles

Logs. When you want to hop a log, throw your body back, yank up on the handlebars, and pedal forward in one swift motion. This clears the front end of the bike. Then quickly scoot forward and pedal the rear wheel up and over. Keep the forward momentum until you've cleared the log, and by all means, don't hit the brakes, or you may do some interesting acrobatic maneuvers!

Rocks and Roots. Worse than highway potholes! Stay relaxed, let your elbows and knees absorb the shock, and always continue applying power to your pedals. Staying seated will keep the rear wheel weighted to prevent slipping, and a light front end will help you to respond quickly to each new obstacle. The slower you go, the more time your tires will have to get caught between the grooves.

Water. Before crossing a stream or puddle, be sure to first check the depth and bottom surface. There may be an unseen hole or large rock hidden under the water that could wash you up if you're not careful. After you're sure all is safe, hit the water at a good speed, pedal steadily, and allow the bike to steer you through. Once you're across, tap the breaks to squeegee the water off the rims.

Leaves. Be careful of wet leaves. These may look pretty, but a trail covered with leaves may cause your wheels to slip out from under you. Leaves are not nearly as unpredictable and dangerous as ice, but they do warrant your attention on a rainy day.

Mud. If you must ride through mud, hit it head on and keep pedaling. You want to part the ooze with your front wheel and get across before it swallows you up. Above all, don't leave the trail to go around the mud. This just widens the path even more and leads to increased trail erosion.

Urban Obstacles

Curbs are fun to jump, but like with logs, be careful.

Curbside Drains are typically not a problem for bikes. Just be careful not to get a wheel caught in the grate.

Dogs make great pets, but seem to have it in for bicyclists. If you think you can't out-run a dog that's chasing you, stop and walk your bike out of its territory. A loud yell to Get! or Go home! often works, as does a sharp squirt from your water bottle right between the eyes.

Cars are tremendously convenient when we're in them, but dodging irate motorists in big automobiles becomes a real hazard when riding a bike. As a cyclist, you must realize most drivers aren't expecting you to be there and often wish you weren't. Stay alert and ride carefully, clearly signaling all of your intentions.

Potholes, like grates and back-road canyons, should be avoided. Just because you're on an all-terrain bicycle doesn't mean you're indestructible. Potholes regularly damage rims, pop tires, and sometimes lift unsuspecting cyclists into a spectacular swan dive over the handlebars.

LAST-MINUTE CHECKOVER

Before a ride, it's a good idea to give your bike a once-over to make sure everything is in working order. Begin by checking the air pressure in your tires before each ride to make sure they are properly inflated. Mountain bikes require about 45 to 55 pounds per square inch of air pressure. If your tires are underinflated, there is greater likelihood that the tubes may get pinched on a bump or rock, causing the tire to flat.

Looking over your bike to make sure everything is secure and in its place is the next step. Go through the following checklist before each ride.

- *Pinch the tires to feel for proper inflation.* They should give just a little on the sides, but feel very hard on the treads. If you have a pressure gauge, use that.
- *Check your brakes.* Squeeze the rear brake and roll your bike forward. The rear tire should skid. Next, squeeze the front brake and roll your bike forward. The rear wheel should lift into the air. If this doesn't happen, then your brakes are too loose. Make sure the brake levers don't touch the handlebars when squeezed with full force.
- *Check all quick releases on your bike.* Make sure they are all securely tightened.
- *Lube up.* If your chain squeaks, apply some lubricant.
- *Check your nuts and bolts.* Check the handlebars, saddle, cranks, and pedals to make sure that each is tight and securely fastened to your bike.
- *Check your wheels.* Spin each wheel to see that they spin through the frame and between brake pads freely.
- *Have you got everything?* Make sure you have your spare tube, tire irons patch kit, frame pump, tools, food, water, and guidebook.

HOW TO USE THESE MAPS   Map Descriptions

Area Locator Map
This thumbnail relief map at the beginning of each ride shows you where the ride is within the state. The ride area is indicated with a star.

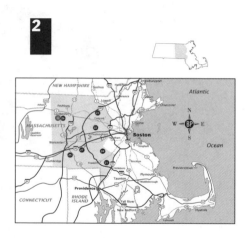

Regional Location Map
This map helps you find your way to the start of each ride from the nearest sizeable town or city. Coupled with the detailed directions at the beginning of the cue, this map should visually lead you to where you need to be for each ride.

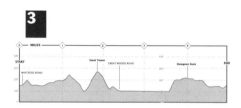

Profile Map
This helpful profile gives you a cross-sectional look at the ride's ups and downs. Elevation is labeled on the left, mileage is indicated on the top. Road and trail names are shown along the route with towns and points of interest labeled in bold.

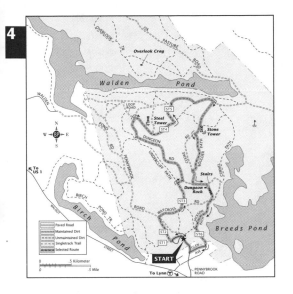

4 Route Map

This is your primary guide to each ride. It shows all of the accessible roads and trails, points of interest, water, towns, landmarks, and geographical features. It also distinguishes trails from roads, and paved roads from unpaved roads. The selected route is highlighted, and directional arrows point the way.

Ride Information *(Included in each ride section)*

☎ Trail Contacts:

This is the direct number for the local land managers in charge of all the trails within the selected ride. Use this hotline to call ahead for trail access information, or after your visit if you see problems with trail erosion, damage, or misuse.

⏱ Schedule:

This tells you at what times trails open and close, if on private or park land.

$ Fees/Permits:

What money, if any, you may need to carry with you for park entrance fees or tolls.

Ⓜ Maps:

This is a list of other maps to supplement the maps in this book. They are listed in order from most detailed to most general.

Any other important or useful information will also be listed here such as local attractions, bike shops, nearby accommodations, etc.

THE MAPS Map Legend

We don't want anyone, by any means, to feel restricted to just the roads and trails that are mapped here. We hope you will have an adventurous spirit and use this guide as a platform to dive into Boston's backcountry and discover new routes for yourself. One of the simplest ways to begin this is to just turn the map upside down and ride the course in reverse. The change in perspective is fantastic and the ride should feel quite different. With this in mind, it will be like getting two distinctly different rides on each map.

For your own purposes, you may wish to copy the directions for the course onto a small sheet to help you while riding, or photocopy the map and cue sheet to take with you. These pages can be folded into a bike bag, stuffed into a jersey pocket, or better still, used with the **BarMap** or **BarMapOTG** (see www.cycoactive.com info). Just remember to slow or even stop when you want to read the map.

Symbol	Description
5	Interstate Highway
8	U.S. Highway
3	State Road
CR 23	County Road
T 145	Township Road
FS 45	Forest Road
	Paved Road
	Paved Bike Lane
	Maintained Dirt Road
	Unmaintained Jeep Trail
	Singletrack Trail
	Highlighted Route
	Ntl Forest/County Boundaries
	State Boundaries
	Railroad Tracks
	Power Lines
	Special Trail
	Rivers or Streams
	Water and Lakes
	Marsh

Symbol	Name	Symbol	Name
✝	Airfield	⚲	Golf Course
✈	Airport	𝄌	Hiking Trail
🚲	Bike Trail	⛏	Mine
⊘	No Bikes	✕	Overlook
⟰	Boat Launch	⚘	Picnic
)(	Bridge	P	Parking
🚌	Bus Stop	✕	Quarry
▲	Campground	(A)	Radio Tower
♨	Campsite	⚐	Rock Climbing
⚓	Canoe Access	▮	School
⊟	Cattle Guard	▬	Shelter
✝	Cemetery	⌐	Spring
⛪	Church	⚱	Swimming
⌂	Covered Bridge	⚑	Train Station
⟿	Direction Arrows	⟁	Wildlife Refuge
⛷	Downhill Skiing	🌲	Vineyard
▯	Fire Tower	◆◆	Most Difficult
⚑	Forest HQ	◆	Difficult
🚙	4WD Trail	□	Moderate
⌇	Gate	●	Easy

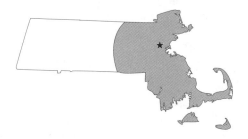

MOUNTAIN BIKE BOSTON

The Rides

1. Circle Boston
2. Lynn Woods Reservation
3. Noanet Woodlands
4. Needham Town Forest
5. Blue Hills
6. Maudslay State Park
7. Ipswich Reservoir Bay Circuit Trail
8. Willowdale
9. Bradley Palmer State Park
10. Georgetown-Rowley State Park
11. Bald Hill Reservation
12. Harold Parker State Forest
13. Dogtown Common
14. Ravenswood Park
15. Chebacco Woods
16. Wompatuck State Park
17. Borderland State Park
18. Freetown State Forest
19. Ames Nowell State Park

20. Myles Standish State Forest
21. F. Gilbert Hills State Forest (Foxboro)
22. Callahan State Park
23. Great Brook Farm
24. Rocky Woods Reservation
25. Purgatory Chasm State Reservation
26. Leominster State Forest
27. Upton State Forest
28. Cape Cod Canal
29. Shining Sea Bikeway

Honorable Mentions

A. Leominster Singletrack
B. Stow Forest
C. Otis

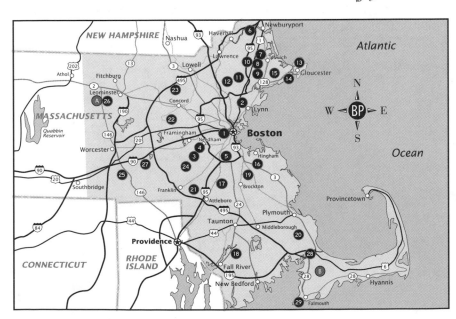

COURSES AT A GLANCE

1. Circle Boston

Length: 8.7-mile loop   **Time:** 1-2 hours
El. Gain: 84 feet   **Difficulty:** Easy

2. Lynn Woods Reservation
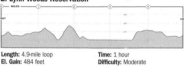
Length: 4.9-mile loop   **Time:** 1 hour
El. Gain: 484 feet   **Difficulty:** Moderate

3. Noanet Woodlands
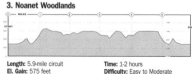
Length: 5.9-mile circuit   **Time:** 1-2 hours
El. Gain: 575 feet   **Difficulty:** Easy to Moderate

4. Needham Town Forest
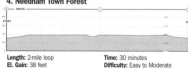
Length: 2-mile loop   **Time:** 30 minutes
El. Gain: 38 feet   **Difficulty:** Easy to Moderate

5. Blue Hills

Length: 3.8-mile loop   **Time:** 30 minutes to 1 hour
El. Gain: 520 feet   **Difficulty:** Moderate to Difficult

6. Maudslay State Park

Length: 3.1-mile loop   **Time:** 30 minutes to 1 hour
El. Gain: 185 feet   **Difficulty:** Easy

7. Ipswich Reservoir Bay Circuit Trail

Length: 4.3-mile loop   **Time:** 1 hour
El. Gain: 154 feet   **Difficulty:** Easy to Moderate

8. Willowdale State Forest
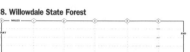
Length: 5.8-mile loop   **Time:** 1 hour
El. Gain: 114 feet   **Difficulty:** Easy to Moderate

9. Bradley Palmer State Park

Multiple Route Options

Length: Up to 30 miles   **Time:** Rider discretion
El. Gain: Depends on route taken   **Difficulty:** Easy to Moderate

10. Georgetown-Rowley State Park

Multiple Route Options

Length: Up to 13 miles   **Time:** 1-3 hours
El. Gain: Depends on route taken   **Difficulty:** Moderate to Difficult

11. Bald Hill Reservation
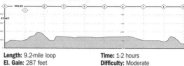
Length: 9.2-mile loop   **Time:** 1-2 hours
El. Gain: 287 feet   **Difficulty:** Moderate

12. Harold Parker State Forest

Length: 5.9-mile loop   **Time:** 1-2 hours
El. Gain: 97 feet   **Difficulty:** Moderate

13. Dogtown Common
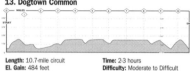
Length: 10.7-mile circuit   **Time:** 2-3 hours
El. Gain: 484 feet   **Difficulty:** Moderate to Difficult

14. Ravenswood Park
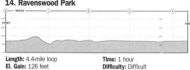
Length: 4.4-mile loop   **Time:** 1 hour
El. Gain: 126 feet   **Difficulty:** Difficult

15. Chebacco Woods
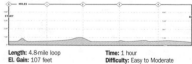
Length: 4.8-mile loop   **Time:** 1 hour
El. Gain: 107 feet   **Difficulty:** Easy to Moderate

16. Wompatuck State Park

Length: 9.6-mile circuit   **Time:** 1-2 hours
El. Gain: 328 feet   **Difficulty:** Moderate

17. Borderland State Park

Length: 3.9-mile loop
El. Gain: 112 feet
Time: 1-2 hours
Difficulty: Difficult

18. Freetown State Forest

Length: 6.9-mile circuit
El. Gain: 417 feet
Time: 1-2 hours
Difficulty: Moderate to Difficult

19. Ames Nowell State Park

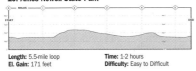

Length: 5.5-mile loop
El. Gain: 171 feet
Time: 1-2 hours
Difficulty: Easy to Difficult

20. Myles Standish State Forest

Length: 11-mile loop
El. Gain: 339 feet
Time: 1-2 hours
Difficulty: Easy to Moderate

21. F. Gilbert Hills State Forest (Foxboro)

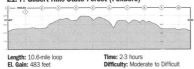

Length: 10.6-mile loop
El. Gain: 483 feet
Time: 2-3 hours
Difficulty: Moderate to Difficult

22. Callahan State Park

Length: 6.5-mile circuit
El. Gain: 352 feet
Time: 1-2 hours
Difficulty: Moderate

23. Great Brook Farm

Multiple Route Options

Length: 11.2 mile out-and-back
El. Gain: Depends on route taken
Time: Rider discretion
Difficulty: Easy to Moderate

24. Rocky Woods Reservation

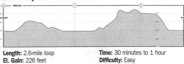

Length: 2.6-mile loop
El. Gain: 226 feet
Time: 30 minutes to 1 hour
Difficulty: Easy

25. Purgatory Chasm State Reservation

Multiple Route Options

Length: 3 miles of trails
El. Gain: Depends on route taken
Time: Rider discretion
Difficulty: Moderate to Difficult

26. Leominster State Forest

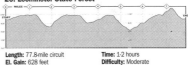

Length: 77.8-mile circuit
El. Gain: 628 feet
Time: 1-2 hours
Difficulty: Moderate

27. Upton State Forest

Length: 6.4-mile loop
El. Gain: 616 feet
Time: 1-2 hours
Difficulty: Moderate

28. Cape Cod Canal

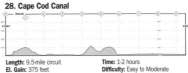

Length: 9.5-mile circuit
El. Gain: 375 feet
Time: 1-2 hours
Difficulty: Easy to Moderate

29. Shining Sea Bikeway

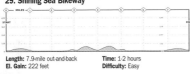

Length: 7.9-mile out-and-back
El. Gain: 222 feet
Time: 1-2 hours
Difficulty: Easy

Boston

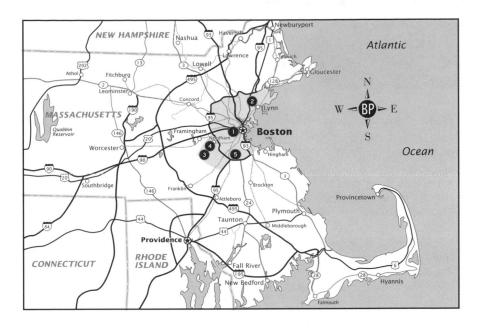

oston is not only the state capital, the home to more than a dozen colleges and universities, and the headquarters for a number of major corporations, it's also a great place to start from if you're looking for exciting mountain biking trails.

Over the course of three and a half centuries, Boston has seen a lot of change. Since day one the city has been, in the words of one historian, "making room for itself." This change started almost immediately when Puritan settlers, displeased with the number of marshes and mudflats they had to contend with, waged war on the glacial mounds that dotted the peninsula. By the end of the 17th Century the marshes and flats were gone, and so too were the majority of the hills used for backfill. Beacon Hill, the loftiest perch in modern-day Boston, was relieved of 60 feet from its top. The filling and leveling frenzy lasted well into this century, to the point where you'd have to be an historian to point out the old Shawmut peninsula.

A cultural hub for all of New England, if not the country, Boston is abound with sights and sounds—and more history, particularly Revolutionary history, than you can shake a stick it. Biking in and around the city presents riders with little difficulty and much in the way of cultural and historic sites, among these: the Freedom Trail, Boston Common, the Museum of Fine Arts (founded 1870), the Paul Revere House, and the Old North Church. Often described as a "walking" city, Boston is equally kind to cyclists. And as you'd expect, by biking you'll be able to see more, do more, and have more time to enjoy it than you ever could by foot or car.

1

Circle Boston

Ride Specs

Start: From the Boston Public Library on Boylston Street
Length: 8.7-mile loop
Approximate Riding Time: 1–1½ hours
Difficulty Rating: Easy, rarely requiring more than basic skill
Terrain: Streets, back alleys, dirt paths, sidewalks, paved cycling and in-line skating trails, stairs, and wide brick expanses
Elevation Gain: 84 feet
Other Trail Users: The entire population of Boston

Getting There

From Outside the City: Follow I-93 to the Massachusetts Avenue exit. With the "Big Dig" currently underway (the Big Dig is a huge construction project that will reroute surface traffic and above-ground traffic to multiple tunnels beneath the city), exit numbers are frequently changing, so keep an eye peeled for the Massachusetts Avenue exit sign. Once you reach Massachusetts Avenue, which is at the end of a looping off ramp with a traffic light in the middle of it, take a right. Follow Massachusetts Avenue until it intersects Boylston Street (about three miles). Take a right on Boylston and follow the road until you reach the Boston Public Library. Boylston is one-way and has parking meters on either side of the road. Eight quarters will get you 2 hours—parking is free on Sundays and holidays. *DeLorme: Massachusetts Atlas & Gazetteer.* Page 73, K-17

Via the Ⓣ : Take the MBTA commuter rail or Orange Line subway to Back Bay Station. The Public Library and the starting point are just up Dartmouth Street.

As you start this ride from the Boston Public Library, stop to appreciate its importance. Established in 1854, it has the distinction of being the first free public library in the United States. Boston, on the other hand, opened for business in 1630. Along this route you'll see most of the landmarks mentioned in this description, including the Charles River, the Hatch Shell, Beacon Hill, Boston Common, Government Center, and more. Take your time pedaling through the city. You'll see more and enjoy it immeasurably.

Centrally located with waterways and roads intersecting in the middle of the town, Boston is still often referred to as The Hub. Bear in mind it took Captain John Smith over 15 years to generate a comprehensive map of Boston proper with its circuitous routes to and from the waterfront. But, like the hubs in your wheels, things are constantly revolving around the city. In fact, Boston is home to some of the most advanced educational institutions in the world, including Harvard University, Massachusetts Institute of Technology, Northeastern University, and the Berklee College of Music.

But while the college-age population of Boston swells each August, the town still boasts its older roots and established celebrities. On part of the trail, at mile 4.0, you'll pass over the Arthur Fiedler Footbridge. Fiedler, who has a plaque and a bust on the other side of road, was one of the most celebrated conductors of the Boston Pops Orchestra. He directed the Pops during all sorts of events including Fourth of July celebrations, winter and summer Esplanade concerts, and other occasions for 50 years until his death in 1979.

The Swan Boats in the Lower Common Pond provide a quieter and more casual atmosphere. For a few bucks local students will paddle you around the shallow lagoon. These boats weave slowly through the water, escorted by numerous ducks and swans. A short distance from the Swan Boats are the bronze statues of the characters in Robert McCloskey's 1941 *Make Way for Ducklings*—a book you can pick up at the library after your ride.

Though having specific attractions on every corner is great, it's also nice to relax by the Charles River or people watch near Faneuil Hall. The Charles is infamous for being a less than clean waterway, but it has become a little more inviting in recent years and is a hotbed of activity from April to October.

Plan your visit to the city in late October and you'll be spectator to one of the world's largest rowing races. The Head of the Charles Regatta attracts hundreds of thousands of people over the weekend of races. Crews from all over the world travel to Boston to row in fierce competition for international recognition. At mile 6.0 you'll pass one of the boathouses used during the regatta. Parking is essentially non-existent during large city events, so knowing your way around by bike is great preparation.

Another huge athletic event that draws even more spectators and participants is the Boston Marathon. Starting in Hopkington, the race follows a fairly straight path all the way into the city, ending right in front of the Boston Public Library. If you come to town in the spring you'll still be able to see the finish line painted on Boylston Street.

If shopping is your thing, both Newbury Street and Copley Place offer upscale boutiques and shoppes to satisfy even the most demanding purchaser. The Prudential Center also has numerous shops, as does Harvard Square, just a few miles away down Massachusetts Avenue. If you're looking to make this detour, keep straight at mile 5.8. Massachusetts Avenue goes straight to Harvard Square. Here you can walk your bike through the ivy-covered brick of Harvard Yard and visit folk bars, noodle emporiums, and more.

Regardless of the path you decide to take through the city, either my route or one you tailor to your particular interests, you won't suffer from a lack of interesting views or fascinating landmarks. Just keep your eyes open and you'll experience history.

MilesDirections

0.0 START at the front door of the Boston Public Library, facing Boylston Street. Take a right on Boylston Street.

0.08 Turn left on Dartmouth Street.

0.1 Turn left on Newbury Street.

0.6 Take a right on Hereford Street. Follow Hereford until it ends at an alley next to Storrow Drive. (Hereford crosses Commonwealth Avenue and Beacon Street before reaching this alley.)

0.8 Take a right down the alley.

1.0 Ride over the footbridge on the left, and take the paved bicycle trail in the direction the ramp feeds you. Follow the Dr. Paul Dudley White Bicycle Path until you see the Hatch Shell.

1.6 The path splits. Continue straight.

1.7 The Hatch Shell is on your right. Continue on the path.

1.9 Ride up the overpass on the left, but take a moment to gander at the city when you reach the top. Cambridge and the Charles River are behind you and Boston is on the right. This bridge heads into the Beacon Hill section of town.

2.1 Take a left at the bottom of the ramp.

2.12 Take a right on Charles Street (one-way to the right).

2.2 Take a left up Revere Street.

2.4 Take a right on Irving.

2.5 Take a left on Myrtle.

2.55 Take a right on Hancock.

2.6 Take a left under the State House arch. There are guards here so just nod politely and coast on through.

2.7 Take a right on Bowdoin.

2.74 Take a left on Beacon.

2.8 Take a left onto Somerset, and ride along it for an instant, and then ride up onto the right-hand curb and onto the brick plaza of the Suffolk University building.

2.81 Ride left diagonally across the small brick plaza to the two sets of stairs. Ride down the stairs.

2.9 Take a right on Tremont Street.

2.95 Go left down School Street.

3.0 Ride left on Washington Street.

3.1 Ride straight across Court and State streets onto the brick Government Center Plaza. Take a sharp left up through the plaza toward State Street and Tremont.

3.3 Continue straight off the curb and down Tremont Street (one-way to the left).

3.5 Granary Burying Ground is on the right. Continue straight.

3.55 Hop the curb at the Boston Common, and take the middle path that starts at the fountain. This path travels diagonally across the common to Charles Street, the road that splits the common into an upper and lower section. There is no bike riding in the lower section.

4.0 Take a right on Charles Street.

4.1 Turn left on Beacon Street. Pass in front of The Bull and Finch Pub (made famous in the television show *Cheers*) at 4.6.

4.2 Take a right at Embankment Road and immediately get on the sidewalk. Go over the Arthur Fiedler Footbridge.

4.4 Take a 90-degree right turn at the bottom of the ramp, and follow to the edge of the Hatch Shell. A small bridge spanning a tiny section of the Charles River is on the left.

4.5 Ride up the steps and over the bridge. Stay on the right-hand section of the path that begins on the other side of the bridge.

5.1 Cross over a bridge to the other path and take a sharp right. Stay to the right when on this path. Hop up the steps of the small plaza and then jump down the steps on the other side. Continue straight.

5.4 A footbridge rises up to the

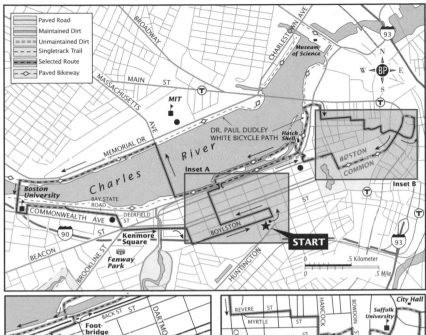

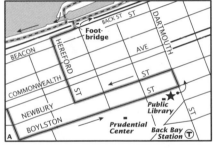

MilesDirections

Massachusetts Avenue Bridge. Go right up this and take a right on the sidewalk next to Massachusetts Avenue.

5.8 Take a left across Massachusetts Avenue, and ride down the other side of the Charles River on the left-hand sidewalk.

6.2 At the "Y" between the sidewalk and the dirt path, take a left down to the water.

6.6 The dirt path joins the sidewalk. Continue straight. The Boston University Crew House is on the left.

6.8 Take a left over the bridge. Be sure to take the left side and to pause for a minute or two in the middle for a premium photo opportunity.

7.0 Take a left on the sidewalk beside Commonwealth Avenue, then turn left on University Road

7.1 Turn right behind the George Sherman Union building on the path parallel to Storrow Drive. Continue straight on to Bay State Road. This travels past Boston University buildings.

7.7 Turn right at Deerfield Street toward Kenmore Square. At Kenmore Square, go across the square and get on the proper side of the road for traffic. Stay to the right on Commonwealth Avenue. Do not enter the tunnel.

8.1 Take a right on Massachusetts Avenue.

8.2 Take a left on Boylston Street.

8.7 Return to the Boston Public Library.

Ride Information

📞 Trail Contacts:
Handled by the **Boston Public Works Department,** Boston, MA (617) 635-7555

🕐 Schedule:
This ride is best when done in the spring, summer, or fall. Early morning or evening hours offer the best views and make getting a parking space easier.

❓ Local Information:
Boston Convention and Visitor's Bureau, Boston, MA (617) 536-4100 • **Massachusetts Bay Transportation Authority (MBTA),** Boston, MA (617) 222-3200

📍 Local Events/Attractions:
Boston Harbor Islands State Park, Boston, MA (617) 727-7676 • **The Wang Center for the Performing Arts,** Boston, MA (617) 482-9393 • **Symphony Hall** (Boston Pops Tickets), Boston, MA (617) 266-1200 • **Boston Red Sox Tickets,** Boston, MA (617) 267-1700 • **Boston**

Bruins and Boston Celtics Information, Boston, MA (617) 624-1000 • **Boston Public Library,** Boston, MA (617) 536-5400 • There are far too many things to see and do in this city that we couldn't possibly list them all.

🚲 Local Bike Shops:
International Bicycle Center, Boston/Allston, MA (617) 783-5804 • **Ace Wheelworks**, Somerville, MA (617) 776-2100 • **Bicycle Bills,** Allston, MA (617) 783-5636 • **Community Bicycle Supply,** Boston, MA (617) 542-8623 • **Central Cycle,** Revere, MA (781) 289-0761 • **Ski Market,** Boston, MA (617) 731-6100 • **Beacon Street Bicycle,** Boston, MA (617) 262-2332 • **Back Bay Bikes and Boards,** Boston, MA (617) 247-2336

🗺 Maps:
USGS maps: Boston South, MA
Any bookstore in the Boston area should have a road map of the city.

Boston's 1990 population was 575,000. That was down from over 800,000 in the 1950s when manufacturing was the city's primary industry.

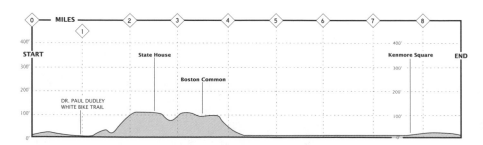

Lynn Woods Reservation

Ride Info

Start: From the parking lot near the Lynn Woods' Superintendent's House
Length: 4.9-mile loop
Approximate Riding Time: 45 minutes due to climbs and terrain
Difficulty Rating: A moderate level trail that has some challenges and some easier terrain. The ride can be extended and made more difficult by linking the other side of Lynn Woods.
Terrain: Primarily singletrack with some fire roads and loose, rocky and sandy doubletrack uphills. Roots and rocks are predominant technical elements.
Elevation Gain: 484 feet
Nearest Town: Lynn, MA
Other Trail Users: Hikers, joggers, snowshoers, and cross-country skiers

Getting There

From Boston: Take U.S. 1 North to the MA 129 / Walnut Street exit, just beyond Saugus. At the end of the ramp, take a right on Walnut Street and follow it to Pennybrook Road. Take a left on Pennybrook Road, which will take you to the parking area and the Lynn Woods Superintendent's House. *DeLorme: Massachusetts Atlas & Gazetteer.* Page 41, B-26

Via the Ⓣ: From North Station take the MBTA Rockport/Newburyport line to Lynn Station. Now on your bike, head west from the station on Market Street toward City Hall. Turn left on North Common Street, and then take the first right onto Franklin Street. Follow Franklin, crossing NH 107 (Western Avenue), and turn left onto Linwood Road. Turn right onto Walnut Street and proceed for one mile to Pennybrook Road. Turn right and follow to the parking area and the Lynn Woods Superintendent's House. (Biking distance from Lynn Station to start: 2.6 miles.)

L ynn Woods can boast being the second largest municipally-owned park in the United States—the largest being Fairmount Park in Philadelphia. Convenient to both the city of Boston and its suburbs to the north and south, the park has over 100 species of birds and other animals within its 2,200 acres—making it an ideal place for nature hikes, biking, and other outdoor activities.

One of the most talked about mountain biking areas in the region, Lynn Woods is made up of typical Eastern singletrack interspersed with a variety of other challenges like sandy, sketchy fire roads and lung-busting climbs. The ride mapped here encompasses the western section of the park and has sections that can test any rider's bike-handling skills.

The eastern section of the park is currently the subject of development talks, but luckily, because of the park's sheer enormity, riding Lynn Woods will be providing marvelous terrain, challenging elevation changes, and breath-taking scenery for a long time to come.

Along this particular ride there are a few items that aren't often found on typical mountain bike trails. For instance, there's Dungeon Rock, a cave that allegedly contains pirate gold. It seems that in 1658 Thomas Veal, a dastardly pirate, sailed his way from the Atlantic Ocean into the Saugus River. Historians believe he had chests full of gold and other ill-gotten treasure on his ship, and he was looking for a place to hide it. After dropping anchor in the river, Veal made his way into Lynn Woods and discovered a natural cave formed in a large rock.

Veal quickly transferred the treasure from his ship to the cave. It is believed that while Veal was in the cave counting his gold, an earthquake struck, entombing Veal in the cave. The legendary site, Dungeon Rock, is one of the most frequented landmarks in the park. An interpretive painting of the Veal, made with the help of a spirit guide, hangs in the Lynn Historical Society's office on Green Street in Lynn.

Another feature of this trail is the Stone Tower. Set on the highest point in Lynn, at 285 feet. Originally built by the Works Progress Administration (WPA), the tower had a wooden roofed structure on top to provide shelter for fire spotting crews who worked inside. Access to the tower is now limited, but you can stand on the stones of the tower and see the Boston skyline and parts of the Lynn waterfront.

Nine miles north of Boston and bordered by the Atlantic Ocean, the city of Lynn encompasses roughly 10 square miles and is home to some 78,000 people. Lynn hosts Olympic figure skating events, offers walking tours of the Lynn Commons, sponsors Earth Day celebrations and clean-ups, and holds and an annual Dungeon Rock tour on Halloween. Lynn's event calendar changes yearly so call the Lynn Chamber of Commerce for the most current schedule. And enjoy the ride through Lynn Woods. It offers a treasure of riding and history.

Ride Information

🕯 Trail Contacts:
Lynn Woods Ranger/Superintendent, Lynn, MA (781) 477-7123
NEMBA, 1-800-57-NEMBA

🕔 Schedule:
The trail is open from May 1 to December 31, dawn to dusk, as long as trail conditions permit. Cross-country skiing and snowshoeing are done during the winter.

❓ Local Information:
Lynn Area Chamber of Commerce, Lynn, MA (781) 592-2900 • **Lynn Historical Society,** Lynn, MA (781) 592-2465

💡 Local Events/Attractions:
Gannon Municipal Golf Course, Lynn, MA (781) 592-8238

🚲 Local Bike Shops:
Lynn Shore Cycle, Lynn, MA (781) 581-2700 • **Hollywood Bike Shop,** Lynn, MA (781) 595-2991 • **International Bicycle,** Allston, MA (617) 783-5804 • **Northeast Bicycles & Skis,** Saugus, MA (781) 233-2664

🅝 Maps:
USGS map: Lynn, MA. • Maps of the reservation are available at the Superintendent's House (781) 477-7123.

MilesDirections

0.0 START the ride with your back to the Superintendent's House. This is the upper level of the parking area with a field to the right. Go straight ahead on Amphitheater Loop, a paved fire road.

0.1 Take a right turn onto ST1, a short section of singletrack at the top of Amphitheater Loop. Take another immediate right between two downed logs onto ST2. ST2 becomes a rooty singletrack and goes upward through the trees.

0.3 Come to a 4-way intersection with Waycross Road and Pennybrook Road. Take a right on Waycross Road, a doubletrack fire road.

0.5 Take a left on the singletrack ST3 that splits like a "Y" from Waycross Road. This trail is rolling terrain with some roots and rocks. It flows downhill and then turns around to the right and climbs straight uphill.

0.8 Take a left at the "T" intersection onto a doubletrack fire road called Dungeon Road.

1.4 Take a right on Loop Road, a loose-surfaced, rocky fire road that climbs up to the Steel Tower.

1.8 At the top there is a clearing with the city of Boston on the right and the Steel Tower on the left. The fire road, still called Loop Road, is level here and circles the Steel Tower (elevation 272 feet). *[**View**. On a clear day the Boston skyline is visible. The tallest buildings in the skyline are the John Hancock Tower and the Prudential Center Building. The Hancock has flat sides and is faced with mirrored windows while the "Pru" is more square and has a top that looks like a small box perched on top of a long skinny box.]* For the descent keep Boston on the right and the Steel Tower on the left and go straight into the woods at a white mark on a trailside tree. The route down is quite quick and has many loose rocks and occasional roots.

1.9 Take a left on the singletrack ST4 at another tree with a white mark on it. Continue riding as the trail begins to level.

2.2 The singletrack splits left and right. Go left on ST5, the blue marked trail.

2.3 Take a right at the "T" intersection onto Great Woods Road.

2.5 Take a sharp right on Cooke Road, another loose and rocky fire road. This climb ends at the Stone Tower. It's a granny-gear climb or even a drag-a-bike climb for anyone not used to loose

gravel combined with a steep grade.

2.7 Arrive at the Stone Tower (elevation 285 feet) and another flat clearing with views of the Atlantic Ocean—an excellent spot for a photo. With the Stone Tower on the left, Cooke Road continues straight ahead and down a steep hill. This downhill can be pretty hairy because of the loose stones and dirt, not to mention the steep grade.

3.1 A large boulder on the left side of Cooke Road marks the entrance to a technical singletrack. Take a left onto this trail, Boulder Path. The trail here has large rocks, some loose sand, and roots. It climbs up quickly and offers a nice challenge after riding some of the more open doubletrack fire roads. Follow this trail (Boulder Path) until it intersects with Cooke Road again.

3.5 Take a left onto Cooke Road and follow it past the boulder down to a "T" intersection.

3.9 Take a left at the "T" intersection onto Dungeon Road.

4.0 Dungeon Road curves to the left and Dungeon Rock is visible on the right. Take a right on the loose, broken rocks and ride up beside Dungeon Rock. This landmark will be on your right. Ahead of you are large, rock steps. During the summer this area is a popular picnic spot, and extreme care should be taken when riding here. The steps can also be treacherous, so less skilled riders may want to carry their bike down the staircase. Keeping the Rock on your right, descend the large stone staircase on your bike. From here back to the parking area is mostly singletrack.

4.2 Come to a 4-way intersection with Waycross Road. Go straight across onto an uphill singletrack (Jackson Path) that winds around a hill with a large pond (Breed's Pond) on your left. The trail climbs fairly steeply and then drops quickly to a clearing with picnic tables and a broken-up patio, visible across the clearing to the right.

4.5 Go straight across the picnic area keeping the patio on your right.

4.55 The trail splits left and right. Take the split to the left onto ST6 and you'll be deposited on a residential street.

4.6 Take a right on Glen Avenue.

4.7 Take a right onto Pennybrook Road and head to the parking area.

4.9 Arrive back at the car.

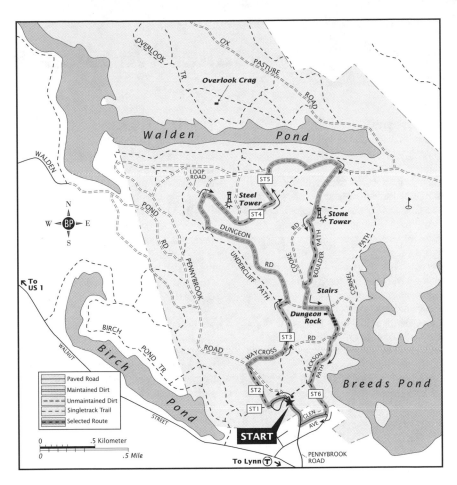

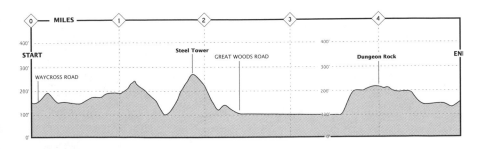

33

3 Noanet Woodlands

Ride Specs

Start: From Caryl Park in Dover next to the ranger station.
Length: 5.9-mile circuit
Approximate Riding Time: 1–1½ hours
Difficulty Rating: Easy to moderate in most locations, with about 10 percent of really difficult riding. Few steep sections but mostly clear of roots and rocks, making the majority of the ride relaxed.
Terrain: Packed-dirt double and singletrack. Some singletrack has loose rocks and roots. Some muddy sections and a few grinding climbs and fast descents
Elevation Gain: 572 feet
Nearest Town: Dover, MA
Other Trail Users: Hikers and equestrians

Getting There

From Boston: Take I-90 West to I-95 / MA 128 South. Head south to MA 109 West (Exit 16). Follow MA 109 west into Westwood, MA. Between Westwood and Medfield, you'll want to look for Walpole Street on the right. Take a right onto Walpole and follow it into the center of Dover. Once in town, take a right onto Centre Street, and then take a right at the "Y" intersection onto Dedham Street. The entrance to the Noanet Woodlands is next to Caryl Park on the right. *DeLorme: Massachusetts Atlas & Gazetteer.* Page 52, A-10

Via the Ⓣ : From South Station take the MBTA Needham line (no Sunday service) to Needham Junction Station. Now on your bike, turn left on Junction Street, and then turn left on Chestnut Street. Turn right on South Street and continue through Charles River Village. South Street becomes Willow Street and then merges into Dedham Street. The entrance to the Noanet Woodlands is next to Caryl Park on the left. (Biking distance from Needham Junction Station to start: 2.9 miles.)

This ride is the second in this guide on property owned and managed by the Trustees of Reservations (TOR). These land reserves are not public and to ride here requires a mountain bike pass or TOR membership. A big reason for purchasing a pass or becoming a member is the way the land is maintained.

The trails, woods, and water here are looked after with extra care and the land sees less use than a state park because membership is necessary for entry. This keeps trail damage to a minimum, often presents a great place for wildlife to flourish, and promotes more camaraderie among trail users. Everyone in the Woodlands is part of the same club trying to preserve the land and therefore feels a sort of link with others in the park.

As with other TOR land, the trails are almost kept like the highways throughout the state. When a hole develops it is promptly filled with dirt or wood chips to prevent further damage. When water from heavy rains creates a flow down the trail, it's diverted by concerned users. The schedule of the park is such that less use is allowed

in wet weather to alleviate damage. In addition, there are special areas just for horse-back riders, like the jumps visible on both the way out and back, that keep heavy impact in one carefully controlled area of the Woodlands.

Ultimately, the paths through the forest evoke a sense of peacefulness. This happens because most of this route takes less attention to navigate but still rolls through beautiful stands of trees, over bubbling streams, and beside glistening ponds. At the end of one path there is a large house across a field of grass and wildflowers. This is as close to civilization as the area gets. Unfortunately, escaping for long periods of time is impossible because the Woodlands are only open during the daytime, and camping is not allowed.

A good portion of this TOR property has not been marked with trail signs, so landmarks are crucial to finding your way around the reserve. The trails are not all jammed together, and turns are clearly visible. In addition, there are reflectors that mark the trail, and those will be noted in the cues wherever they appear.

Beside Noanet Woodlands is the Hale Reservation. This land is not TOR or public land but does have some riding within its borders. Robert Hale, in the early 1900s, purchased the 1,200 acres for use as a camping and recreation area for Boy Scouts and other groups. The land is now conservation land, meaning it cannot be developed. It's home to a day camp during the summer months, which precludes a lot of in-season riding. During the other times of the year the two trail systems can be linked for about 10 to 15 miles of riding.

For the amount of money you'll spend on a TOR riding tag ($15 in 1999), you'll get more than that back in good riding and scenery. The tags are good at any TOR property that allows bikes, and the pass is good for the whole year. So take a trip out to Dover and get away from the pressures of life with a ride into the Woodlands.

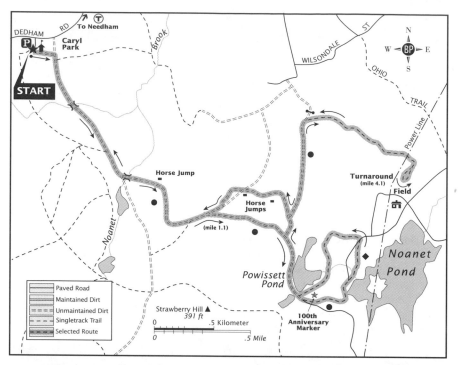

Paved Road
Maintained Dirt
Unmaintained Dirt
Singletrack Trail
Selected Route

Strawberry Hill ▲
391 ft

0 .5 Kilometer
0 .5 Mile

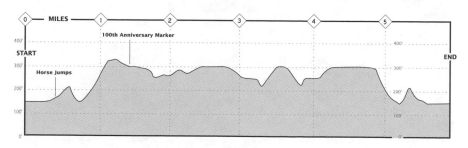

MilesDirections

0.0 START the ride at the right side of the ranger cabin in the dirt parking lot off of Dedham Street in Dover. Ride straight into the woods to the right of the cabin, and take a right onto the wide dirt doubletrack trail.

0.1 Take a left at the "Y" intersection and follow the woodchip-covered doubletrack uphill as it winds left through the trees.

0.3 Take a left down a short singletrack section to a wooden bridge and a stream. Cross over the bridge and proceed uphill on some rooty singletrack.

0.4 At the "T" intersection, take a left and ride on hard dirt doubletrack to the Noanet Woodlands entrance.

0.5 At the sign for the reserve take a left uphill on doubletrack, and then take a right following the blue reflector.

0.6 At the horse jumps and the three-way intersection, take a right up the thinner doubletrack and follow to the top.

0.63 Take a right at the top onto a doubletrack access road. This trail also winds uphill and has a few very sandy sections.

0.8 Take a left into the woods on a more technical doubletrack trail.

1.0 Take another left on the thin doubletrack trail. It will have fewer roots and is a little wider than the trail that you turned from.

1.1 At the "Y" intersection go right, downhill.

1.3 Remain right and follow the trail as it winds downhill.

1.4 At the pond, look for the 100th Anniversary Marker, dedicated by Mr. & Mrs. G.H. Lovell. It is just off to the left of the main trail that bisects the pond. Keep the marker on the left and ride straight ahead up a gradual grade.

1.5 At the split in the trail, take a left.

1.6 Remain to the left past the trail turn and then take a right uphill on thinner doubletrack.

1.7 There is a clearing in between two trails. Remain riding diagonally across the clearing and enter the woods on the other side.

1.9 At the "T" intersection, go right.

2.0 Take a left up a brutally technical section. This is one area that has not been attended to by TOR management.

2.1 At the top of the hill, take a left. There is a large rock on the left. It's a suitable place for a snack, a Gu packet, or just a rest. Now continue beside the rock on the thin path.

2.2 The trail gets steeper and flies downhill in the clearing that was crossed earlier. Watch out for the tree that is over the last ridge before the bottom.

2.4 At the "T" intersection at the bottom of the hill, take a right.

2.5 Take a right up a singletrack trail.

2.6 Take a right on more singletrack at the Woodlands boundary. Follow this trail straight.

2.9 After crossing the big clearing and riding into the woods on the singletrack, take a right downhill. This winds around to the clearing again.

3.1 At the clearing and the downhill, take a left. Again watch for the tree on the other side of the last ridge.

3.15 At the "T" intersection at the bottom, take a left back to the pond.

3.3 At the other side of the pond, take a right on the doubletrack fire road.

3.8 At the fire gate, take a right on the undulating singletrack trail.

3.9 Remain to the left on the main singletrack trail.

4.1 Turn around at the "T" intersection and head back to the fire road. If you took a right at this "T" there would be a large field and a private residence at the end of the trail. A left brings riders to another park boundary.

4.4 Back at the fire gate and doubletrack fire road, take a left.

4.45 Take a right on the doubletrack trail and head uphill past the horse jumps.

4.5 At the top of the hill, take a right and then another right again after a moment.

4.7 Cross over the stream at fire gate.

4.75 Take a right back onto a dirt doubletrack and follow it until the ranger's cabin is in sight.

5.9 Take a left into the parking lot to end the ride.

Ride Information

☎ Trail Contacts:
Noanet Woodlands, c/o Trustees of Reservations, Dover, MA (508) 785-0339 or (781) 821-2977 or *www.the trustees.org*

🕐 Schedule:
The park is open most of the year. The trails are closed when cross-country skiing conditions exist and also when the trails are muddy. This is usually from March 1 through April 30.

$ Fees/Permits:
There's no fee, but you must be a Trustees member or have a mountain bike pass. For a mountain bike pass or to become a TOR member, call the general headquarters in Beverly, MA at (978) 921-1944.

❓ Local Information:
South Shore Chamber of Commerce, Quincy, MA (617) 479-1111

Metro South Chamber of Commerce, Brockton, MA (508) 586-0500 • **MBTA,** Boston, MA (617) 222-5000 – *for train information on the Needham commuter rail*

♥ Local Events/Attractions:
Cardinal Spellman Philatelic Museum, Weston, MA. (781) 894-6735 • **Davis Museum & Cultural Center,** Wellesley, MA. (781) 283-2051

🚲 Local Bike Shops:
Town & Country Bicycles, Medfield, MA. (508) 359-8377 • **Harris Cyclery,** West Newton, MA. (617) 244-1040 • **International Bicycle,** Newton, MA. (617) 527-0967

Ⓝ Maps:
USGS maps: Medfield, MA • Maps are available from the TOR Regional Office, (781) 821-2977

Needham Town Forest

Ride Specs

Start: From the main parking lot off of Central Street

Length: 2-mile loop

Approximate Riding Time: 30 minutes

Difficulty Rating: Easy to moderate because of the ride length. A fairly level grade with wide doubletrack in most areas. Some sections are difficult in wet weather.

Terrain: Various doubletrack with some roots and rocks. Minimal uphills and downhills. A few short sections of singletrack and rutted sections of doubletrack fire road. One area of technical rocks and tight singletrack.

Elevation Gain: 38 feet

Nearest Town: Needham, MA

Other Trail Users: Hikers, joggers, and walkers

Getting There

From Boston: Travel I-90 West to I-95 South. Take I-95 to MA 135 West (Exit 17). MA 135 becomes Great Plain Avenue. Take a left onto Central Avenue and keep an eye open for the parking area on your left. It will appear after you pass Marked Tree Road. Start your ride from this parking area. *DeLorme: Massachusetts Atlas & Gazetteer.* Page 40, N-10

Via the ⓣ: From South Station take the MBTA Needham line (No Sunday service) to Needham Station. Now on your bike, take a right on Great Plain Avenue (MA 135). Turn left on Marked Tree Road until it runs into Central Avenue. Turn left on Central Avenue and proceed to the parking area on the left. (Biking distance from Needham Station to start: 1.5 miles.)

Shorter and less technical than most of the rides in the book, the Needham Town Forest loop is perfect for riders just breaking into the sport. The trails within the 200-odd-acre park run the gamut from plain-Jane fire roads to frighteningly rocky sections. But no one specific element dominates. One readily noticeable feature of the forest is how wet it gets—or rather, stays. Even though this ride was mapped after a bout of heavy rain, the drainage is typically slow and most water crossings have boards and logs across them all year long. Though the wet conditions can make for some insect-laden riding, the soggy soil provides a substantial foundation for hundreds of native plants and flowers. It's these conditions that draw the many hikers and naturalists to the area.

Adjacent to the park is the town of Needham, only 10 miles southwest of Boston about 30,000 strong. Incorporated in 1711, Needham remains a quite vibrant community, with numerous clubs and activities for its residents. Chances are though, if you hear someone speak of Needham, Massachusetts, it's usually with regard to carnations. And why? One of the town's most famous residents was Denys Zirngiebel, the first person to successfully cultivate the French perennial carnation in America.

Originally from Switzerland, Zirngiebel came to the United States in 1855. After working for a number of years developing plant species at the Harvard Botanical Gardens, Zirngiebel moved to Needham in 1864 and bought 35 acres on South Street. His spacious property allowed him to practice his craft while entertaining such luminaries as Henry Wadsworth Longfellow. (It's believed that Longfellow's poem "To The Charles River" is based, in part, on the view of the Charles River from Zirngiebel's porch.)

A Frenchman by the name of Alegotune encouraged Zirngiebel to develop carnations in the States and Zirngiebel took the challenge. The growing conditions required for healthy carnations necessitated that Zirngiebel development a revolutionary floriculture technique. By inventing and perfecting a forced hot water heating system for greenhouses he was able to grow plants in optimum conditions year-round. With this new system, Zirngiebel bred carnations and other flowers to the point where his work was nationally recognized. His enterprise led to the start of the commercial carnation business in America.

It was during this period that Zirngiebel grew a variety of pansy that would ultimately land him his 15 minutes of fame. The Giant Swiss Pansy—Zirngiebel's creation—was adopted as the Needham town flower, and Zirngiebel would become renowned as the Pansy King. Zirngiebel received numerous awards and accolades for his efforts—in fact, his pansies were delivered daily to the White House. To look at it, the Giant Swiss Pansy really is a giant, with blossoms that can reach four inches in diameter. Zirngiebel died in 1905 at the age of 76 and his memory is honored each year by the Needham Historical Society during the Spring Pansy Festival.

MilesDirections

0.0 START the ride facing the back of the parking area. The benches are on the left. In heavy rain, the whole area will be flooded. Straight ahead is a rutted doubletrack fire road (FR1). Go straight on this doubletrack.

0.3 Make a hairpin left turn on ST1, which is a wide singletrack that climbs steeply.

0.4 The trail becomes thinner singletrack and runs downhill to a wet area. Logs and branches are often placed here to minimize damage. Ride across the bottom and pedal back up the hill.

0.5 Trail comes to a "T" at more doubletrack. Go right on DT1.

0.6 The trail veers to the right and runs downhill behind some houses.

0.8 Come to a wet section marked with branches. Cross over the water and stay right on a short doubletrack uphill (DT2).

0.9 Singletrack (ST2) leads left into the woods toward a large rock. This is the tightest and most technical the trail will get during this ride. *[Option. To avoid this section, continue straight on the doubletrack (DT2) and you'll*

meet up with FR1.] Ride to the right of the large rock. The trail crosses a ridge and then drops quickly to your right and winds down a hill into more water.

1.0 Cross over a seasonal stream and go up the slight grade, which will meet up again with the doubletrack (DT2).

1.1 Go right on the doubletrack fire road (FR2).

1.3 FR2 comes to a "T." Take a right and follow FR1 up a slight grade.

1.45 Take a right on a section of rutted doubletrack (DT3) and follow it downhill, while looking carefully to the left for a singletrack trail up into the woods.

1.5 At the bend in DT3, take a left-hand turn into the woods on winding singletrack (ST3). This trail climbs uphill and is littered with rocks and roots. Follow ST3 until the end, where you'll pop back out on DT3.

1.7 Take a right on DT3.

1.8 Take a right on FR1 and follow it back to the lot.

2.0 Arrive at your car.

Ride Information

Trail Contacts:
Needham Park and Recreation Commission, Needham, MA (781) 449-7521 • **Needham Recreation Information Line,** Needham, MA (781) 444-7212 • **NEMBA,** Action, MA 1-800-57-NEMBA or *www.nemba.com*

Schedule:
The trail is open as long as trail conditions permit. Cross-country skiing is done during winter.

Local Information:
Needham Town Offices, Needham, MA (781) 455-7500 • **Newton-Needham Chamber of Commerce,** Newton, MA (617) 244-5300 • **Arnold Arboretum,** Jamaica Plain, MA (617) 524-1717

Local Events/Attractions:
The Pansy Festival, held the last Saturday of April, Needham. MA (781) 455-8860 • **Needham Historical Society,** Needham, MA (781) 455-8860

Local Bike Shops:
International Bicycle, Newton, MA (617) 527-0967 • **Belmont Wheel Works,** Belmont, MA (617) 489-3577 • **Dedham Bike,** Dedham, MA (781) 326-1531

Maps:
USGS map: Framingham, MA • The park map (revised in 1983) is available at the Needham Town Offices, (781) 455-7500.

Needham is fairly small, but it offers much more than a yearly flower festival. Though Needham Forest is the only place in town to welcome mountain biking, Needhamites have created multiple recreation fields around town. There's an outdoor facility called the Fit Trail that has 20 distinct workout stations and 32 specific exercises for those interested in working up a sweat. For more relaxed recreation, the town has a series of Bocce/Shuffleboard/Horseshoe courts off Great Plain Avenue as well as the Rosemary Pool Complex—a pond that offers swimming, sailing, and other water sports. Needham is a pleasant little town whether you're searching for special garden items or looking for a little ride in the woods.

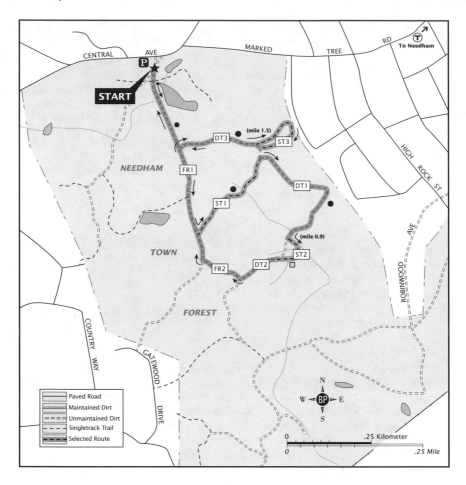

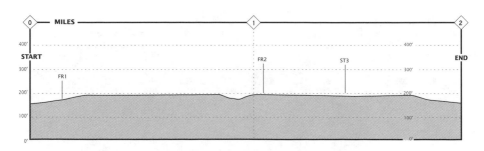

Blue Hills

5

Ride Specs

Start: From the main parking area by Houghton's Pond
Length: 3.8-mile loop (up to 20+ miles of trails of additional riding within the 7,000-acre park; see map for details)
Approximate Riding Time: 30 min.–1 hour
Difficulty Rating: The trails in this ride are moderate to difficult because of the climbing involved. The terrain is only tough to navigate when it becomes loose and rocky, near the end of the ride.
Terrain: Paved fire roads, doubletrack, and singletrack. Abundant loose rocks with medium-sized drop-offs. Moderate amount of packed dirt.
Elevation Gain: 520 feet
Nearest Town: Milton, MA
Other Trail Users: Hikers and equestrians

Getting There

From Boston: Travel south on I-93 to MA 138 (Exit 2). Follow MA 138 to the first right, Hillside Street. Hillside leads to the main Blue Hills parking area—about a mile and a quarter away. Begin the ride at the parking lot entrance farthest away from the concession area and restrooms. *DeLorme: Massachusetts Atlas & Gazetteer:* Page 53, C-20

Via the ⓣ: From South Station, take the MBTA Franklin Line to Readville Station. Now on your bike, turn left onto Valley Parkway eastbound. Turn right onto Blue Hill Avenue (MA 138). Turn left onto Summit Road (gated) at the three-way intersection with Canton Avenue. Turn left on Wolcott Path. Pick up the chapter route at Trail Junction 1085 (that's mile 1.4 in the cues) by making a right on Puddle Path. (Biking distance from Readville Station to start: about 1 mile.)

The Blue Hills Reservation is one of the premiere mountain biking areas in Eastern Massachusetts because of its extensive trail system and varied terrain. Bordered by six cities and towns, the reservation encompasses about 7,000 acres, a good portion of which is available for mountain biking. Blue Hills is called a reservation because it is a forest reserve with the land owned by the state. The state governs the activities within the reserve and polices the property.

Depending on your biking stamina and skill, it's easy to loop a 12 to 20 mile ride together or to do a brief jaunt like the one detailed here. The trails on the Hills are of rooted Eastern singletrack with small rocks, sand, and even some fairly large boulders that test your agility and nerve. Aside from some challenging terrain, the most difficult aspect of Blue Hills is the climbs. They range from paved fire roads to rutted doubletrack to snakes of rooty singletrack that rise up to the sky.

Blue Hills is a prime place to work your way from smoother, dirt doubletrack to severely hardcore rides that traverse some of the toughest technical terrain in the area. On this ride you'll pilot your bike to the top of Great Blue Hill (the tallest point on the coast of Massachusetts at 635.5 feet) and then cruise back down to nearly sea level.

Local riders praise the Blue Hills' varied terrain as much as they do the management's efforts to keep the Hills in great shape. Local groups like the New England Mountain Bike Association (NEMBA) have been very active in repairing

trail damage and leading bike rides. In very severe weather, including heavy rains and snow, NEMBA endorses a riding ban at Blue Hills to help preserve the trails.

If you're looking for off-season exercise or even some diversions during your visit to the area, Blue Hills boasts a nice swimming area in Houghton's Pond, as well as fishing holes, picnic areas, tennis courts, and ball fields. During the winter Blue Hills turns into the Blue Hills Ski Area. Open during daylight hours, the ski area offers moderate to easy trails with affordable ticket prices. Aside from Wachusett Mountain in Princeton, Massachusetts, this is the closest downhill skiing to Boston.

In addition, the Blue Hills Trailside Museum in Milton offers a look at the natural history of the area. Inside are live animal exhibits and presentations on the habitats found in the Blue Hills. The Massachusetts Audubon Society runs the museum and admission is $3 for adults.

Since you're in the area, it might be of interest to know that former President George Bush was born in Milton on June 12, 1924, but sources cannot confirm that he ever rode a bike though the Blue Hills Reservation. Enjoy your ride at Blue Hills. It may not lead you to the White House, but on this ride you'll certainly be King of the Hill.

Ride Information

🕯 Trail Contacts:
Metropolitan District Commission, Milton, MA (617) 698-1802 • **NEMBA,** Action, MA 1-800-57-NEMBA

🕙 Schedule:
The reservation opens for mountain biking on April 15 each year and closes on December 31.

❓ Local Information:
South Shore Chamber of Commerce, Quincy, MA (617) 479-1111

🔦 Local Events/Attractions:
Blue Hills Trailside Museum, Milton, MA (617) 333-0690—*open year-round on*

Tuesdays through Sunday, 10 a.m. to 5 p.m. • **Blue Hills Ski Area,** Milton, MA (617) 828-7490

🚲 Local Bike Shops:
Dave's Bike Infirmary, Milton, MA (617) 696-6123 • **Norwood Bicycle Depot,** Norwood, MA (781) 762-2112 • **Quincy Cycle,** Quincy, MA (617) 471- 2321

Ⓝ Maps:
USGS maps: Norwood, MA • There are detailed maps for mountain biking, hiking, and horseback riding available at the ranger station across the road from the main parking area.

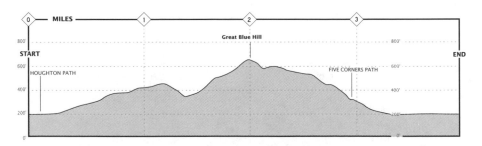

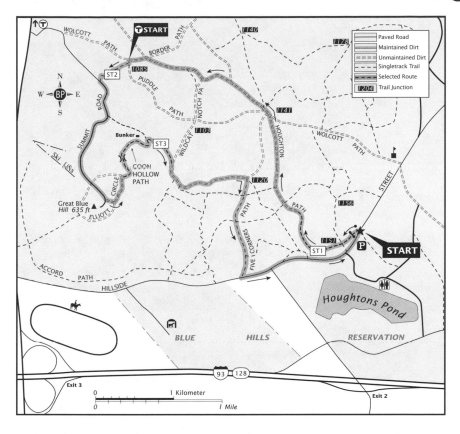

MilesDirections

0.0 START at the second parking lot entrance facing Hillside Street, and ride across the road to the fire gate. Take a left through the fire gate and ride uphill on ST1, a wide singletrack trail.

0.2 At this "Y" go right up the Houghton Path Extension and then remain straight on Houghton Path.

0.7 Houghton Path comes to a "T" intersection. Take a left on Wolcott Path, a wide doubletrack trail.

1.4 Take a left on Puddle Path and an immediate right on ST2, a singletrack that winds uphill briefly, but quite steeply.

1.5 Take a left onto Summit Road, a paved access road.

2.0 This is the top of Great Blue Hill. There is a thin doubletrack, Eliot Circle, on the left. Follow this trail around to the left.

2.2 Take a right on Coon Hollow Path and follow it downhill slightly. Cross over a stone bridge and come upon a stone building (2.4).

2.5 Take a right down ST3—the singletrack path located across from the wide side of the stone building. This trail begins on loose shale and travels over multiple rocks, with a few moderate drop-offs.

2.6 At a three-way doubletrack intersection, join up with Wildcat Notch Path and ride down to the right.

2.9 Take a right down Five Corners Path and bounce along down the hill. Follow this trail to the very bottom.

3.2 Nearly at the bottom you can hear the cars on Hillside Street, but the trees and brush obscure your view. Carefully ride down over the final big rocks and drop-offs to Hillside Street. Five Corners Path empties from a 30-degree angle onto Hillside, so keep your brakes ready.

3.3 Take a left on Hillside Street and spin back to the parking lot.

3.8 Take a right into the parking lot.

North of Boston

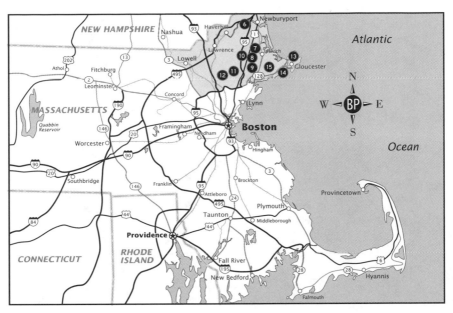

orth of Boston is a pleasant mix of riding conditions. Many of the trails wind through great stands of trees interspersed with lower foliage. The only detriment to this area is the occasional horse or deer fly. While riding each of the trails for this book, I encountered these pests only in this area. Still, it's worth slathering on bug spray because the North rides offer a broad variety of terrain and elevations that challenge all rider levels. There are also numerous beaches up here and the seafood is fantastic. Just be warned that the water temperature in the ocean off the North Shore is typically about 10 degrees cooler than the waters south of Boston or on Cape Cod.

Maudslay State Park

6

Ride Specs

Start: From the entrance to the field across the street from the Maudslay State Park parking area

Length: A number of trails lie within the 3.1-mile outer loop. There are 476 acres here.

Difficulty Rating: Easy because the trails are mostly wide, dirt doubletrack. There are a few dips and rises, but the ride is essentially level.

Terrain: Packed dirt doubletrack with an occasional rock or root. A minimal amount of singletrack and some grass fields. Mulch and bark are present on some trails to fill in holes and deter erosion.

Elevation Gain: 185 feet

Nearest Town: Newburyport, MA

Other Trail Users: Hikers and equestrians

Getting There

From Boston: Take I-93 North to I-95 North. Continue on I-95 to MA 113 East (Exit 57). Go east on MA 113 for about half a mile, and turn left onto Noble Street. Follow signs to the park and leave your vehicle in the dirt lot near the park headquarters. ***DeLorme: Massachusetts Atlas & Gazetteer:*** Page 19, K-20

audslay State Park offers a relaxing place to ride with a number of natural sights not found in other parts of the state. First is the Merrimack River. This waterway travels down from the middle of New Hampshire to Massachusetts where it takes a left turn toward the Atlantic Ocean. The roaring river forms part of the western border of the park and is a hotbed of activity in the warmer months.

The side of the river makes an ideal place for a picnic, and it's also a prime location to see another fascinating sight, the American bald eagle. Our national bird nests here during the winter months. A portion of the park remains closed to the public so that this majestic creature can reside undisturbed. Trail maps indicate where the nesting areas are, and riding trails intentionally follow the contours of the closed areas just so trail users can peer into the bird's habitat.

Another fantastic sight is the assortment of flowers that are present all over the park. In May and June a number of plants come into bloom, making the fields a natural canvas for their colors. The Greenhouse Area also has a number of hedges cut in the shape of a labyrinth. It's a nice area through which to stroll—bikes are not allowed within the bushes.

In addition to these features, the park offers a calm, flowing surface that could be ridden on a hybrid without difficulty. Some trail surfaces are loose, but it's not slippery gravel or sand. A mulch and wood-chip layer helps maintain the paths and keeps water from rutting the trails. The hill grades here are very moderate, and the only real steep area, the Punchbowl, is closed to all visitors. The Punchbowl is a natural kettle hole,

a deep round depression in the earth, that has been overused by visitors. Park management is in the process of restoring the area. The walls of the hole drop about 40 feet.

Other sites in the park include a rose garden, the Azalea Swamp, and a number of groves of trees. In fact, one of the largest naturally-occurring stands of mountain laurel in the state grows within the eagle's protected nesting area. One final note on this park. Park officials make sure that the rules of the trail are followed and that protected areas remain untrammeled. They have been known to levy $50 fines for violations of the posted rules. This is a relaxed atmosphere for riding—perfect for the family—so please save your thrashing for elsewhere. Considerate riders out to see some natural wonders will enjoy Maudslay State Park.

Ride Information

🛈 Trail Contacts:
Maudslay State Park, Newburyport, MA (978) 465-7223 • **NEMBA,** Acton, MA 1-800-57-NEMBA or *www.nemba.org*

🕐 Schedule:
The park is open year-round from 8 a.m. to sunset. The American Eagle Habitat is closed from November through March.

❓ Local Information:
Greater Newburyport Chamber of Commerce, Newburyport, MA (978) 462-6680

💡 Local Events/Attractions:
Newburyport Whale Watch, Newburyport, MA (978) 465-9885 •

Historical Society of Old Newbury (Cushing House Museum), Newburyport, MA (978) 462-2681 • **Custom House Maritime Museum,** Newburyport, MA (978) 462-8681

🚲 Local Bike Shops:
Aries Sports & Bikery, Newbury, MA (978) 465-8099 • **Cycle Re-Cycle,** Haverhill, MA (978) 372-0313 • **Bay Road Bikes,** South Hamilton, MA • (978) 468-1301

🅝 Maps:
USGS maps: Newburyport, MA Trail maps are available at Maudslay State Park Headquarters, (978) 465-7223.

MilesDirections

Though there are distinct pathways throughout Maudslay State Park, many of them intersect and entwine. The park's small size makes it highly manageable for a self-guided tour. In fact, detailing a particular route among the multiple options would be of little use to the reader.

Riding through Maudslay allows you to lighten up on your gear load because you'll never be more than a mile from the parking area. You may want to bring beverages and snacks, but there's probably little need to bring a whole array of tools or more than one tube.

But for such a short ride, Maudslay State Park has a variety of riding surfaces and a few really nice views. As you cut into the park from the parking area you can just let the scenery take you back in time. Aside from titanium bikes and gadgets, the most technological thing you'll encounter in this park is a baby stroller.

This park is for beginning riders and those who just want to take it easy. If you gaze across the field at the entrance, you'll see that the terrain is fairly level. The pathways here are hard-packed dirt doubletrack, paved side-walk-width paths, and a smattering of easy, rolling singletrack. Even the hills here can be ridden by nearly all levels, and most can be tackled in the middle ring. The most difficult section of this ride is the short singletrack path that connects the main path with the doubletrack along the river's edge.

Toward the back of the park, sandwiched between the field and the Merrimack River is the eagle nesting area. To view these birds during their annual visit to the park, check with a park ranger for recent sightings and locations. Then, ride along the smooth dirt path to the back of the field. Follow this well-worn singletrack path around to the right and you'll be riding along the boundary of the eagle's area.

The land at Maudslay used to be part of a private estate where poets and artists came to get back in touch with nature. The estate currently has over 70 rooms and is located adjacent to the main paved path. Maudslay State Park isn't the largest park, but it offers elements not found in other rides and can be enjoyed by the whole family.

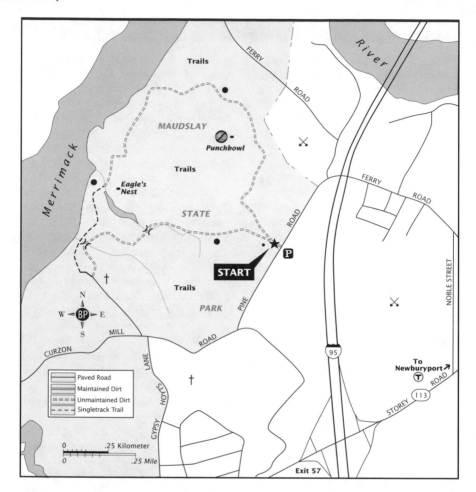

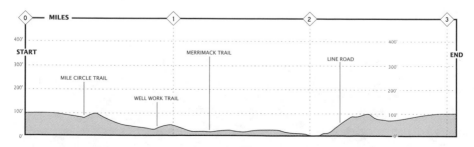

Ipswich Reservoir Bay Circuit Trail

Ride Specs

Start: From the Ipswich Light Department, off Massachusetts 1A

Length: 4.3-mile loop, with options to connect to a host of other singletrack and doubletrack trails

Approximate Riding Time: Advanced Riders, 30 minutes; Intermediate Riders, 45 minutes

Difficulty Rating: Technically easy to moderate due to occasional muddy section or climb. Physically easy to moderate due to short mileage and some moderate climbing. More strenuous climbs along Prospect Hill.

Terrain: Mostly doubletrack and singletrack, some dirt roads. Consists of mostly smooth-running singletrack and doubletrack, but there are a number of wet, muddy patches. Some sections of singletrack can be rocky or washed out.

Elevation Gain: 154 feet

Nearest Towns: Ipswich, MA

Other Trail Users: Hikers, runners, equestrians, picnickers, and hunters (in season)

Getting There

From Boston: Take U.S. 1 North to MA 128 East toward Gloucester. Take the exit for MA 1A North (Exit 20). Drive north on MA 1A, past downtown Ipswich and past the new high school. At Mile Lane (on the left), you'll see a classic piece of American architecture, the Clambox. This little restaurant, literally shaped like a giant clam box, has been serving famous Ipswich fried clams since 1935. Two-tenths of a mile past the Clambox, you'll see the entrance to the Ipswich Utilities Department on your left (the large transfer station is hard to miss). Take that left, and park on the side of the road.

Via the Ⓣ: Take the MBTA Newburyport line from North Station to Ipswich Station. Now on your bike, head east from the station on Market Street. Turn left on to MA 1A (High Street). Pedal north on MA 1A, past downtown Ipswich and past the new high school. At Mile Lane (on the left), you'll see the Clambox Restaurant. Two-tenths of a mile past the Clambox, you'll see the entrance to the Ipswich Utilities Department on your left (the large transfer station is hard to miss). Take that left, and start your ride here. (Total distance from Ipswich Station to start: 2.5 miles.)

DeLorme: Massachusetts Atlas & Gazetteer. Page 30, D-3

This little gem just off Massachusetts 1A in Ipswich serves up a great sampling of coastal New England-style mountain biking. There's a fairly intricate network of marked and unmarked trails snaking through the 500 acres here, but with major roads bordering all four sides, it's next to impossible to get lost.

Dow Brook and the Dow Brook Reservoir are fed by the southern run-off from Prospect Hill, a 270-foot glacial drumlin that actually sits on the south side of Rowley. This 90-acre parcel once served as pasture land for early settlers and actually housed a small family-owned ski area from 1948 until the mid 1970s. The Massachusetts Department of Environmental Management purchased the land in

1995. On a clear day, this perch atop Prospect Hill offers wonderful views of Rowley and beyond, including Cape Ann, the Isle of Shoals in New Hampshire, and Mount Agamenticus in Maine.

Cut along the hillside, the Bay Circuit Trail is narrow and rolling, a real joy for beginner and advanced riders alike. The climb to the top, however, can be washed out with numerous loose rocks strewn about, and requires refined bike handling skills and strong legs. The lower portion of this trail network, between Bull Brook and Dow Brook, is a mix of wetland and second- and third-growth forests, with numerous stone walls serving as a reminder that this was once farmland. (Cyclists are asked to refrain from riding here when this lower area is extremely wet.)

The Bay Circuit Trail eventually connects these trails behind the Ipswich Reservoir to neighboring Willowdale State Forest. However, there is enough variety in this small maze of trails—many of which actually form concentric circles, like water drops— to keep most off-road cyclists happy exploring for the better part of an afternoon. Many of the trails run around or over another small upland ridge located just southeast of Prospect Hill, between Bull Brook and Dow Brook. The power lines that run straight through the property also serve as an unmistakable landmark. Keep your eyes peeled for wildlife, which ranges from deer and woodchucks to birds of prey. One caveat: if you ride in the late fall, during hunting season, wear blaze orange or other bright colors, and equip your bike with a bell.

Ride Information

Trail Contacts:
Bay Circuit Alliance, Andover, MA (978) 470-1982 • NEMBA, Acton, MA 1-800-57-NEMBA or www.nemba.org

Schedule:
Year-round, dawn to dusk. Mountain biking is permitted anytime except when the trails are extremely wet (use your good judgment).

Local Events/Attractions:
The Bay Circuit Trail. The Bay Circuit Alliance is a non-profit organization whose ultimate goal is to establish a trail through conserved green space for passive recreation from Newbury to Duxbury, Massachusetts—roughly 180 miles long.

Restaurants:
Spud's, Rowley, MA (978) 948-7551 • The Choate Bridge Pub, Ipswich, MA (978) 356-2931

Books:
The Bay Circuit Guide to Walks In and Around Ipswich, produced by the Ipswich Bay Circuit Trail Committee, available at Ipswich Town Hall.

Local Bike Shops:
Skol Ski Shop, Ipswich, MA (978) 356-5872 • Bay Road Bikes, Hamilton, MA (978) 468-1301

Maps:
USGS maps: Ipswich, MA

MilesDirections

0.0 START from your car, heading west (away from Massachusetts 1A) on the thin paved road toward the Ipswich Water Department building.

0.1 Just past a "Pedestrians Crossing" sign, you'll see a well-groomed path heading off to the left. Take it.

0.2 Arrive at a small holding dam and a small pond, the Bull Brook Reservoir. You'll also see a split in the trail, marked by a Works Progress Administration sign from the 1930s, a legacy of the Great Depression and Franklin Roosevelt's New Deal program. The main route continues straight, but we're going left, on a thin ribbon of singletrack that runs along this small reservoir.

0.4 The singletrack flows back into the main trail and comes to a "T" intersection. Go left.

0.5 Ignore the trail that veers off to the right.

0.6 Come to a well-defined "T" intersection and go right. Look for the Bay Circuit Trail white blazes. (A left turn at this intersection would take you over a dilapidated old bridge across Bull Brook and follow the Bay Circuit Trail across some athletic fields on Mile Lane, across Linebrook Road, and eventually into Willowdale State Forest.)

0.7 Bear left at the fork in the trail and follow the white blazes. A right-hand turn will complete a short loop and bring you back to the power lines and Dow Brook Reservoir.

0.9 *[Option. On the right, a steep, loose single-track climbs a small hill. If you're feeling up to it, this short, tough climb is rewarded with a fast descent on the other side. It eventually spills back into the Reservoir Trail that leads to Dow Brook Reservoir.]* We're going to stay straight here, along the Bay Circuit Trail.

1.2 Come to a wide, potentially confusing intersection. Staying right here puts you on the main Reservoir Trail. We're staying left to create a larger loop. Although the trail can be messy here (thanks to local ATV riders), especially during mud season, it is well marked with white blazes.

1.4 A couple of trails will veer off to the left, and head west toward Massachusetts 1A in Rowley. We're staying straight.

1.5 Cross underneath power lines.

1.6 Come to a small, sturdy wooden bridge that crosses Dow Brook. Immediately afterward, you'll see a narrow singletrack intersection. This is the Dow Brook Trail, which we'll revisit on the last leg of this loop. For now, we're heading straight along the Bay Circuit Trail toward Prospect Hill, the only out-and-back portion of this ride.

1.8 Come to a wide-groomed doubletrack. Take a quick right and left. The jog in the trail is well marked with double white blazes.

1.9 Start a gradual climb along the hillside. You'll see a big house to the right, and the trail follows the property line over a small feeder stream and into some nice rolling singletrack. Prospect Hill is up to your left.

2.1 Come to a "T" intersection. You'll see a farming operation at the base of the hill to your right. We're turning left. Assume you're best climbing position for this rutted drainage trail.

2.3 Finish this short grunt of a climb to the top of Prospect Hill. You'll see a large white concrete water tank and spotlight tower. There are also some smaller singletrack trails veering off to the left to explore. But for this ride, this concludes the "out" section, and now we begin heading back, pedaling down the same trail we just climbed.

2.5 Look to the right, before you reach the bottom of the hill, for the Bay Circuit Trail. Take that right. *[Option. If you sustain a mechanical in this area, this is a good escape hatch. You can head straight down this hill and onto Massachusetts 133 in Rowley. Take Massachusetts 133 east to Massachusetts 1A south to get back to your car.]*

2.7 Back on the Bay Circuit Trail, pass the house and the small feeder stream once again.

2.8 Return back to the main doubletrack. Take a quick right and left, putting you on the trail toward Dow Brook.

2.9 At Dow Brook, just before the wooden footbridge, take a left on the narrow Dow Brook Trail.

3.3 Come to a well-defined trail intersection. To the left are "No Hunting" and "Private Property, No Trespassing" signs. Go right. Shortly afterward, you'll come to another intersection, and you again want to turn right.

3.6 At the "Y" intersection, bear left. You might be able to see the reservoir in front of you from here through the trees.

3.7 Spill into another trail, with the Dow Reservoir in plain sight in front of you. Take a

MilesDirections *continued*

right, hop over a small concrete culvert, and come to another wide "Y" intersection. We're going to finish this loop by bearing left (or east) here, hugging the south shore of the reservoir. *[Option. For those with more time, a right will put you back on the Reservoir Trail, heading South.]*
4.0 For one last morsel of singletrack, look for a small trail entrance to the left just as you come to a stand of pine trees that lines the reservoir. This little singletrack parallels the doubletrack, and both head back to the parking area.

4.2 Pop back onto the power lines, coming into a gravel path that flows into a slim paved road that crosses the dam at Dow Reservoir. Here the singletrack spills back into the trail as well. Take a right onto the paved road, go underneath the power lines, and then make a quick left. Just before taking that left, you'll see the trailhead in front of you where you began this loop.
4.3 Arrive back at the parking area.

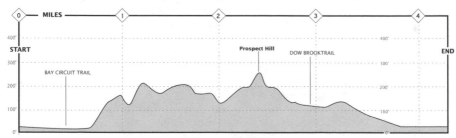

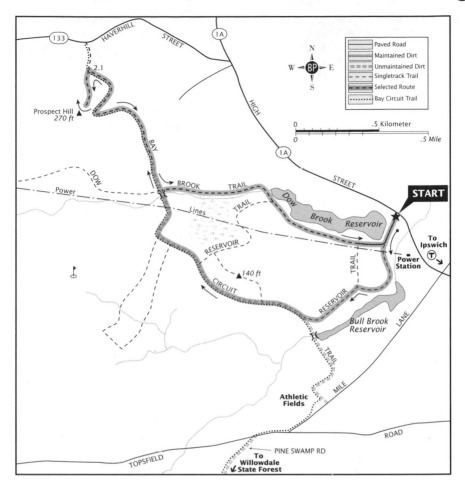

8

Willowdale

Ride Specs

Start: From the No. 42 signpost on Ipswich Road, 1.8 miles east of U.S. Route 1

Length: 5.8-mile loop, with options to connect to a host of other singletrack and doubletrack trails, particularly to the west on U.S. Route 1, on the Hood Pond section of the forest. (Note: Take care in crossing this busy two-lane highway.)

Approximate Riding Time: Advanced Riders, 30 minutes; Intermediate Riders, 45 minutes

Difficulty Rating: Technically easy to moderate due to occasional singletrack, with tricky root and rock crossings. Physically easy to moderate due to short mileage and little climbing. However, the smooth doubletrack invites friendly competition, and therefore can be more demanding.

Terrain: Improved dirt roads, doubletrack (often wet), and singletrack. Consists of mostly smooth-running doubletrack, but there are a number of tight, twisty singletrack sections. Low-lying areas can be muddy during spring, fall, and following heavy rains.

Elevation Gain: 114 feet

Nearest Towns: Ipswich, MA

Other Trail Users: Hikers, runners, equestrians, loggers, and hunters (in season). Boating and fishing occur on the 100-acre Hood Pond.

Getting There

From Boston: Take U.S. 1 North to Topsfield. Go east on Ipswich Road (which becomes Topsfield Road in Ipswich, a quaint but befuddling New England custom) for 1.8 miles. The park entrance, on the north (left) side of the road, is obvious though not well marked. To the south (right) is Bradley Palmer State Park. The trail is marked by a chained fence and a signpost with the No. 42 on it. *DeLorme: Massachusetts Atlas & Gazetteer.* Page 30; F-1

Via the Ⓣ : From North Station take the MBTA Newburyport line to Ipswich Station. Now on your bike, head west from the station on Topsfield Road for 3 miles to the entrance on the right. The trail is marked by a chained fence and a signpost with the No. 42 on it.

Nestled between Bradley Palmer State Park and Georgetown-Rowley State Forest is the lesser-known and perhaps under-appreciated Willowdale State Forest. "Willow Dale" was once part of the late Bradley Palmer's 10,000-acre North Shore estate. The wealthy lawyer and industrialist donated the Willowdale land to the state in 1923 and 1944, leasing back the 100-plus acres surrounding his mansion—which still stands on the grounds of Bradley Palmer State Park.

Divided into two sections—the Pine Swamp area to the east of U.S. Route 1 and the Hood Pond / Cleaveland Farm areas to the west—the 2,400-acre forest features roughly 40 miles of trails. Mountain bikers with the time and stamina can connect Bradley Palmer and Georgetown-Rowley through Willowdale via the Bay Circuit Trail. Because of its hub nature, Willowdale has become popular among equestrians, nature lovers, walkers, and other trail users—these trails have become a favorite of a local off-road running club. Luckily the forest is popular among wildlife as well.

Whitetail deer, owl, partridge, wild turkey, fox and coyote sightings are not uncommon. Be mindful that this is a working forest, used for logging and hunting (in November and December). Exercise caution if you're riding during hunting season or near logging areas.

The amenities at Willowdale are few, but there is a fair amount of off-road riding, if you know where to look. Beginners may want to stay on the well-marked and well-traveled perimeter trail, a wide doubletrack covering roughly 11 miles. You'll want to beware of wide wet sections during spring and fall, or following heavy rains. The mud on these trails can be both deep and slick.

Our loop covers about six miles through a thick forest that features an Eastern hardwood mix of maples and oaks, and evergreens such as Eastern white pine and Canadian hemlock. The trails are predominantly wide, cruising doubletrack, but this route incorporates a few grin-inducing sections of singletrack that feature tricky, off-camber roots, rock gardens, and stone walls for obstacles. The loop is a popular spot for beginner mountain bikers looking to graduate to the intermediate level. On Monday evenings during daylight savings time, a local shop, Bay Road Bikes on Railroad Avenue in Hamilton, hosts a beginner mountain bike ride that often visits these trails after pedaling through Bradley Palmer.

Ride Information

🌙 Trail Contacts:
Bradley Palmer State Park, Topsfield, MA (978) 887-5931

🕐 Schedule: Year-round

❓ Local Information:
NEMBA, Acton, MA 1-800-57-NEMBA or www.nemba.org

💡 Local Events/Attractions:
The Bay Circuit Trail. The Bay Circuit Alliance is a non-profit organization whose ultimate goal is to establish a trail through conserved green space for passive recreation from Newbury to Duxbury, Massachusetts—roughly 180 miles long.

🍴 Restaurants:
The Weathervane Tavern, Railroad Avenue, Hamilton, MA (978) 468-2600

The Choate Bridge Pub, Ipswich, MA (978) 356-2931

📖 Books:
The Bay Circuit Guide to Walks In and Around Ipswich, produced by the Ipswich Bay Circuit Trail Committee, available at Ipswich Town Hall.

🚲 Local Bike Shops:
Skol Ski Shop, Ipswich, MA (978) 356-5872 • **Bay Road Bikes**, Hamilton, MA (978) 468-1301

🅝 Maps:
USGS maps: Ipswich, MA • **Willowdale /Cleaveland Farm State Forest Trail Map** – *available from the Bradley Palmer State Park, (978) 887-5931.*

MilesDirections

0.1 START shortly after heading north onto the wide doubletrack trail, at the top of a small, rooty rise, you'll see a well-defined singletrack on the right that climbs a short hill. This tight little stretch of single-track trail is known by locals as Jim Black No. 1. There are lots of twists and turns, off-camber roots, and the occasional log hop.

0.3 Reach a trail intersection. Head straight across, angling slightly to the right, but staying on the sin-gletrack.

0.4 The singletrack spills into a "T" intersection and wide doubletrack. Head left. Ignore the trail that turns left almost immediately after this intersection and head straight.

0.5 A small ribbon of singletrack veers to the right. Take this shortcut.

0.8 The singletrack spills back into the doubletrack. Almost immediately, you'll see a trail intersection. Stay right.

1.2 While on the doubletrack, you'll cross a low water area with numerous dead trees. This section can be muddy, especially after a heavy rain or in the early spring and fall.

1.3 Ignore the trail that veers off to the right. Stay left. Blue and red triangles will point you in the right direction. Wide sweeping turns let you carry some speed and boost your heart rate.

1.7 Come to a multiple intersection, and take a hard left. Ignore both right-hand turns. Look for trail No. 13 marker, and follow the red triangle.

2.0 Come to another important intersection. The main trail veers to the right, up a loose gravel hill. Stay straight, on a less-defined dirt path. Follow the white triangle.

2.1 The main path bears left, but keep an eye to the right. There's a rooty patch of singletrack that shoots off here, over an old stone wall and into the woods. This smooth, curvy singletrack is marked with big blue triangles.

2.4 Pop back out onto a main section of doubletrack and bear left, over an earthen bridge through a marshy area (note the beaver dam on the left) and into the back of a cornfield (which is leased by the state). At the top of a short knoll, you'll see a farm and the occasional car motoring along Linebrook Road.

2.7 Note the ridgeline you're on, with short but sharp drops to either side into surrounding wet-lands.

2.9 Keep an eye to the left. The main doubletrack continues straight, but a choice piece of single-track—well-traveled but not marked—is on the left. This stretch is known as CB No. 1 after Christine

Beard, a local cyclist who may not have built the trail, but apparently uncovered it.

3.2 The singletrack crosses a doubletrack. Deep ruts can swallow the front wheel of an unsuspecting rider. The doubletrack is also a popular equestrian trail, so be attentive of your surroundings as you head straight across.

3.3 The trail turns sharply to the right, up a short incline, over another old stone wall and down a loose S-turn. Notice the blue triangles. A few hun-dred feet past the bottom of the S-turn, you'll come to a singletrack intersection, a T-stop. Go left, and follow the orange dots.

3.5 Hug a small streambed on your right, and then follow the sweeping singletrack.

3.6 Punch over a small stone wall and drop into the doubletrack again. Go right.

3.7 Ignore the singletrack to the left.

3.8 Come to another split in the trail. Stay right.

4.6 Come to a well-marked intersection with a num-ber of white trail markers and several white triangles pointing to the right. Follow them and spill into another trail (look for trail marker No. 5).

4.8 Come to another intersection. This is a poten-tially confusing part of the trail. In front of you is a large tree, with a carved sign pointing to the right (or north), indicating the direction to Hood Pond and Georgetown. You can go left, right, or straight here. Our route goes straight. Go up a brief incline and fol-low the trail as it bears left. Shortly, just past a large hardwood tree, you'll see a subtle singletrack on the right, which is cut into a small hillside. This is known as Jim Black No. 5. Take it.

5.0 Come to the first of two huge fallen logs, a chance to test your trials skills.

5.1 Reach another stone wall. Cross it. At the bot-tom of a short drop, bear right.

5.2 The singletrack empties into another double-track trail. Go right and head toward the parking area.

5.4 You'll be back at that odd intersection. At the first V, bear left and then head straight through an intersection on the main trail.

5.5 Ignore the trail coming in from the right.

5.7 You may notice a sharp left turn. Ignore it. Shortly afterward, a doubletrack veers to the right. Ignore that as well. Follow the blue, red, and white trail markers.

5.8 Cross a poured concrete bridge and swoop to the left. Immediately, you'll come to a "T" intersec-tion. Bear right, up a short incline, past the entrance to Jim Black No. 1 (which is now on your left) and head down to the parking area.

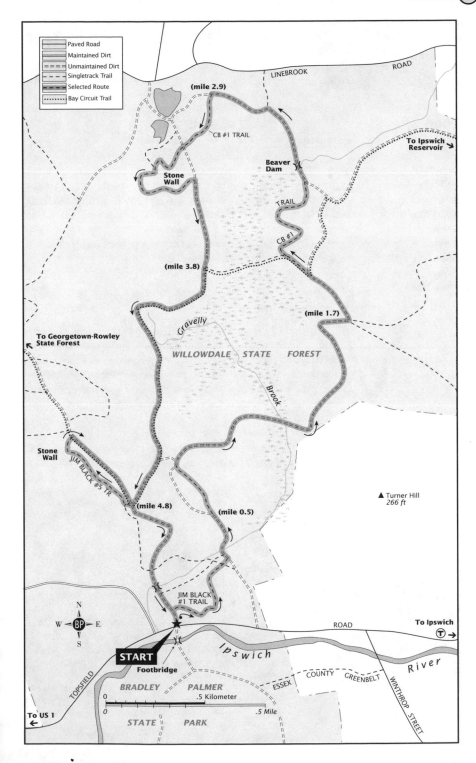

Paved Road
Maintained Dirt
Unmaintained Dirt
Singletrack Trail
Selected Route
Bay Circuit Trail

(mile 2.9)

LINEBROOK
ROAD

CB #1 TRAIL

To Ipswich
Reservoir →

Beaver
Dam

Stone
Wall

TRAIL

CB #1

(mile 3.8)

(mile 1.7)

Gravelly

To Georgetown-Rowley
State Forest

WILLOWDALE STATE FOREST

Brook

Stone
Wall

JIM BLACK #5 TR

▲ Turner Hill
266 ft

(mile 4.8)

(mile 0.5)

JIM BLACK
#1 TRAIL

N
W ⊕ E
S
BP

ROAD

To Ipswich
Ⓣ →

START

Footbridge

Ipswich

River

BRADLEY PALMER

ESSEX COUNTY GREENBELT

WINTHROP STREET

TOPSFIELD

0   .5 Kilometer
0   .5 Mile

STATE PARK

To US 1
←

Bradley Palmer State Park

Ride Specs

Start: From the park headquarters, just off Asbury Street

Length: 35 miles of trail within 723 acres

Difficulty Rating: Easy to moderate because the trails are mostly dirt doubletrack with some hard climbs and loose surfaces

Terrain: Packed-dirt doubletrack bridle trails, sandy fire roads, paved access roads, and some thin, rocky doubletrack trails

Nearest Town: Topsfield, MA

Other Trail Users: Hikers and equestrians

Getting There

From Boston: Take U.S. 1 North to Ipswich Road in the town of Topsfield. Follow Ipswich Road east toward the town of Ipswich and look for a state park sign at the light at Asbury Street. Take a right on Asbury Street and then a left into the park. Drive around the circle to the park headquarters and the main parking area. *DeLorme: Massachusetts Atlas & Gazetteer:* Page 30, F-1

V isiting Bradley Palmer State Park is like stepping into the old Wild West. Horses constantly ride by, and their owners often yell out a greeting, as if they're pleased to see cyclists on the trails with them. In fact, most of the people I met on horseback were happy to talk about the trails and showed interest in our sport. This familiarity makes encounters less adversarial and allows everyone to enjoy themselves.

It's important to remember that many horses are uneasy around mountain bikes. Please take the time to ask the horseback rider what he or she would like you to do. The park ranger informed me that most horseback riders and their horses here are used to mountain bikes, but if they ask you to dismount your bike, please do so.

As far as the trails go, they are nearly as friendly to bikes. The hard dirt surfaces allow tires to hook up well, and climbing is just a matter of moving the cranks. The hills here, Blueberry and Moon Hill, are not too tall. They have some nice paths downhill that resemble wide singletrack and wind around the face of the hills. There are a few trails on the face of Blueberry Hill that are overgrown with thorn bushes, but downhill options are plentiful, and the majority of the riding is on wide, flat doubletrack.

The flat doubletrack covers over 720 acres and winds around the park like a giant maze. The main thing to understand is that most of the trails intersect with another path or the access road at some point. Residential streets surround the entire park. This makes getting lost possible, but not too likely. The park's trail maps are fairly accurate and were last updated in 1998.

While motorized vehicles are not allowed here in the summer, the park does allow snowmobiles in the winter, as well as cross-country skiing. Camping is not allowed, but there are a few picnic areas and restrooms in three locations. And the main insect that will pester riders during late spring and most of the summer is the horsefly. Park management puts out horsefly traps to control the bugs, but the only way to prevent bites is to ride very fast or slap them dead the instant they land on your body. Fortunately, the flies I saw, and killed, were small in size and the bites didn't hurt too badly.

Overall, Bradley Palmer State Park is a good basic ride that makes a great stepping stone for the learning rider. The hills are fairly easy and the technical elements are less prevalent than in other rides in this guide. So mount your steel steed and ride on over to Bradley Palmer.

Ride Information

🖉 Trail Contacts:
Bradley Palmer State Park, Topsfield, MA (978) 887-5931 • NEMBA, Acton, MA 1-800-57-NEMBA or www.nemba.org

🕒 Schedule:
The park is open year-round, with horseback riding and mountain biking in the warmer months and cross-country skiing and snowmobiling in the winter.

❓ Local Information:
Ipswich Visitor Information Center, Ipswich, MA (978) 356-8540

💡 Local Events/Attractions:
Ipswich River Wildlife Sanctuary, Topsfield, MA (978) 877-9264 • Topsfield Fair Topsfield, MA (978) 887-5000

⌀ Local Bike Shops:
The Bicycle Shop, Topsfield, MA (978) 877-6511 • Bay Road Bikes Inc., South Hamilton, MA (978) 468-1301 • Aries Sports & Bikery, Newbury, MA (978) 465-8099

Ⓜ Maps:
USGS maps: Ipswich, MA • Trail maps are available from the Bradley Palmer State Park Headquarters, (978) 887-5931.

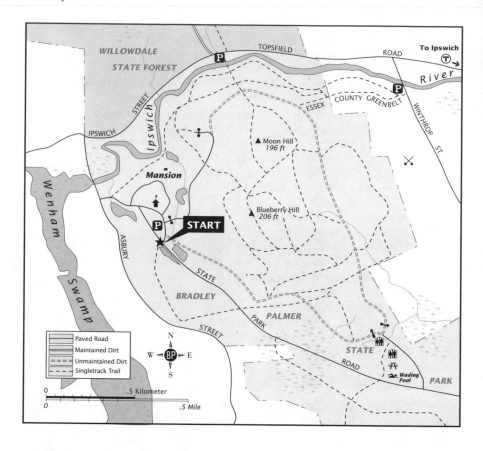

MilesDirections

This park is a maze of trails. When linked they add up to over 30 miles of doubletrack, paved access roads, and dirt fire roads. To make a fair-sized loop through the park, take a left at the first fire gate from the park headquarters. Follow the paved fire road to a "Y" intersection with a dirt fire road and go right on the dirt fire road. Follow this dirt road to the first wide doubletrack trail on the right.

This doubletrack climbs up Moon Hill and then connects with Blueberry Hill. Ride the numerous trails around the tops of these hills and then come down on the southern side.

This will present a network of trails that weave toward the picnic areas and the Wading Pool.

Remember to keep the paved access road on the right to reach the southern border of the park. Once at the southern edge, cross the access road and head back to the park headquarters. The trails will cross the access road twice and finally arrive on Asbury Street with a short (less than a half-mile) road ride back to the main entrance. Follow the road at the entrance back to the parking area and the park headquarters.

Georgetown-Rowley State Park

Ride Specs

Start: Start the ride at the fire gate on the left at the end of Pingree Farm Road
Length: 13 miles of trails within 1,200 acres
Difficulty Rating: The trails in Georgetown-Rowley are moderate to difficult because of the loose soil, the climbs, and the abundant roots.
Terrain: Rocky and rooty singletrack as well as smooth, dirt and sand doubletrack
Nearest Town: Georgetown, MA
Other Trail Users: Hikers, equestrians, and ATVs

Getting There

From Boston: Take I-93 North to I-95 North. Continue on I-95 North to Exit 53. At the exit, head north on MA 97, toward Boxford and Georgetown. After a couple miles begin looking on the right for Pingree Farm Road. Take a right on Pingree Farm and follow it to the end. The entrance to Georgetown-Rowley State Forest is at the small dirt parking lot.
DeLorme: Massachusetts Atlas & Gazetteer. Page 29, C-27

Georgetown-Rowley State Forest's 1,200 acres stretch across Interstate 95, almost squarely between the towns of Georgetown and Rowley. The forest is a mix of all-terrain vehicle trails and bridle/bicycle paths, making for an interesting mix of riding surfaces. Most of the time riders will want to stay on the singletrack, but the rolling fire roads offer a different challenge with their loose surface and gradual hills.

One of the first things you'll notice when you head onto the singletrack in the northwest corner of the forest is the trail maintenance. The New England Mountain Bike Association (NEMBA) has done a lot to make the bike trails more rideable and challenging. Volunteers have also spent time building a long wooden bridge and clearing downed trees—two features that make riding here a lot more enjoyable. Few mountain bikers like to wade waist-deep through a river or climb over numerous tree limbs in the midst of a great ride.

This is one of the few parks in this part of the state to allow all-terrain vehicles, and this creates an added element of danger to riding. Although the motorcycles and four-wheelers are supposed to stay on fire roads they are often seen cruising in all parts of the forest. Remain alert and be prepared when you hear an approaching vehicle. Get as far off the trail as possible. Trail misuse can be reported to the officials at Bradley Palmer State Park as they oversee Georgetown-Rowley as well as two other state recreation areas.

Wildlife and hunters are two other dangers in the forest. Listed on the signs at the trailhead are the seasons for hunting and type of wildlife being hunted. The state has posted a small disclaimer on the sign warning that the forest is a multi-use facility and hunting can take place via special permits at other times than those listed. As far as wildlife is concerned, the sign lists a black bear hunting season, which would suggest that these animals can be found in the forest.

Georgetown-Rowley offers many challenges within its boundaries, but to expand your riding experience, you may want to link this ride with other trails in other local parks. Just southeast of this forest is Willowdale State Forest, a park about as big as Georgetown-Rowley with plenty of singletrack and a prohibition on motorized vehicles. Head south a little and you'll be able to link up with the multiple bridle trails at Bradley Palmer State Park. If you want, the ride can add up to more than 50 miles.

Ride Information

🕿 Trail Contacts:
Georgetown-Rowley State Forest, c/o Bradley Palmer State Park, Topsfield, MA (978) 887-5931 • **NEMBA,** Action, MA 1-800-57-NEMBA or *www.nemba.com*

🕓 Schedule:
The park is open year-round. Hunting is allowed in the fall and winter, except on Sundays.

❓ Local Information:
Ipswich Visitor Information Center, Ipswich, MA (978) 356-8540

💡 Local Events/Attractions:
Crane Beach, Trustees of Reservations, Ipswich, MA (978) 356-4351 • **Heard House and Whipple House Museums,** Ipswich, MA (978) 356-2811

⊕ Local Bike Shops:
Bay Road Bikes Inc., South Hamilton, MA (978) 468-1301 • **Aries Sports & Bikery,** Newbury, MA (978) 465-8099

ⓝ Maps:
USGS maps: Ipswich, MA • Trail maps are available at Bradley Palmer State Park Headquarters, (978) 887-5931.

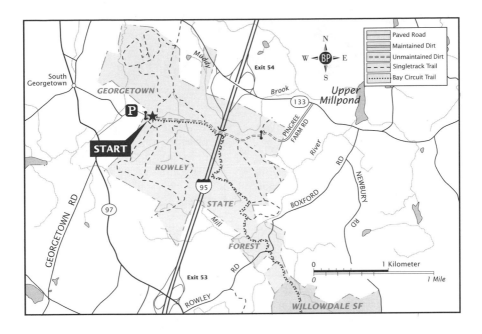

MilesDirections

Georgetown-Rowley State Forest has myriad trails in a fairly small area. The singletrack trails maintained by NEMBA are marked with light blue rings on the trees and the doubletrack trails are clearly marked on the Georgetown-Rowley State Forest Trail Map. To create a 13-mile loop, start out at the left-hand fire gate and take your first three lefts. These will take you from the fire road to a doubletrack dirt trail and then to the singletrack portion of the park. Once on the singletrack, follow around the perimeter of the forest until you intersect with doubletrack trails. These will cross Interstate 95 and connect with the lower portion of the forest. Continue your exploring and enjoy the ride.

11 Bald Hill Reservation

Ride Specs

Start: From the trailhead off Middleton Road, 1.5 miles from Endicott Road

Length: 9.2-mile loop, with options to connect to numerous singletrack and doubletrack trails

Approximate Riding Time: Advanced Riders, 45 minutes; Intermediate Riders, 1½ hours

Difficulty Rating: Technically moderate due to numerous rooty and rocky sections, in addition to stream crossings. Physically moderate, depending on your pace, due to mileage and some moderate climbing. The technical nature of this trail provides a complete workout.

Terrain: Technical singletrack and well-marked doubletrack. An intriguing mix of geology, ranging from hard, rocky soils to thick bogs. The corresponding plantlife and wildlife is also remarkably diverse.

Elevation Gain: 287 feet

Nearest Towns: Boxford, MA

Other Trail Users: Hikers, runners, bird-watchers, picnickers, cross-country skiers, and snowshoers. Fishing and trapping are permitted within the portion managed by the state Division of Forest and Parks. Hunting and trapping are forbidden in the Wildlife Sanctuary.

Getting There

From Boston: Head up U.S. 1 to I-95. Take the Endicott Road exit (Exit 51, the same exit for Masconomet Regional High School). Take a left turn at the end of the exit and cross over the highway. At 0.2 miles, take a right onto Middleton Road. At 1.5 miles, you'll come to the entrance to Bald Hill Reservation on the left-hand side. The parking area is marked with an information board (featuring a relief map and some information on the area) and a fire lane gate. To avoid getting towed or ticketed, be sure not to park in front of the fire lane gate. *DeLorme: Massachusetts Atlas & Gazetteer:* Page 29, G-26.

This loop through the Bald Hill Reservation features a variety of riding rarely matched anywhere. Aside from the absence of long climbs and descents, this mosaic of preserved woodland boasts an incredible array of trail conditions, from challenging rock-garden singletrack to smooth, fast, hard-parked dirt trails. Beginner riders may want to opt to stay on the wider trails, though the narrow cobblestone singletrack provides an excellent opportunity to improve your bike-handling skills while taking you to the less-traveled corners of the reservation. These trails can, however, be as rigorous as they are beautiful, and the nine-mile loop may seem longer as a result. Bring plenty of water, and don't be bashful about taking a breather and enjoying your surroundings every now and then. The sights include a phenomenal mix of plantlife ranging from ferns and honeysuckle to tall pines and eastern hardwoods such as red oak, mountain maple and shagbark hickory. In terms of wildlife, you might come across red-shouldered hawks, barred owls, waterfowl, grouse, turkey, mink, otter, rabbits, fox, and deer.

The 1,624-acre Bald Hill Reservation is actually an assemblage of three parcels held by three separate owners: the state Division of Forest and Parks, the state Division of Fisheries and Wildlife, and the Essex County Greenbelt Association. Within the reserve you'll find the Boxford State Forest and the John Phillips Wildlife Sanctuary (named after the nationally recognized conservationist who bought 120

acres near Crooked Pond and donated it to the state in 1922). Mountain bikers and nature lovers alike should be thankful for the efforts in the early 1960s of a dedicated few with the Essex County Greenbelt who went to court to block plans to develop Bald Hill into 99 house lots. The Greenbelt won in court, and the land was subsequently purchased by the state.

The two state agencies and Essex County Greenbelt manage the property jointly through the Boxford State Forest Advisory Council. Essex County Greenbelt has also formed the Friends of Bald Hill Reservation organization, which helps maintain this amazing network of trails. Mountain biking advocates, such as local members of the New England Mountain Bike Association, have worked closely with land managers and other groups here to preserve the rights of off-road cyclists, so visitors are asked to respect the "No Biking" signs posted on some of the more environmentally sensitive trails. Some of these signs are posted seasonally, depending on the amount of rainfall. But even with seasonal trail closures, there is no shortage of choice riding options within the Bald Hill Reservation.

Ride Information

📞 Trail Contacts:
Massachusetts Division of Forests and Parks (978) 369-3350 • **Massachusetts Division of Fisheries and Wildlife** (978) 263-4347 • **Essex County Greenbelt**, Essex, MA (978) 768-7241

🕐 Schedule:
Year-round

❓ Local Information:
Friends of Bald Hill Reservation, c/o Essex County Greenbelt, Essex, MA (978) 768-7241 • **NEMBA**, Acton, MA 1-800-57-NEMBA or www.nemba.org

🍴 Restaurants:
Topsfield House of Pizza, Topsfield, MA (978) 887-9642

📖 Books:
Bay Circuit Guide to Walks In and Around Boxford, produced by the Boxford Trails Association, available at the Town Clerk's Office (978) 887-0806.

🚲 Local Bike Shops:
The Bicycle Shop, Topsfield, MA (978) 887-6511

🅝 Maps:
USGS maps: Ipswich, MA; Lawrence, MA • **Bald Hill Reservation Trail Map**, Essex County Greenbelt – *available from the Essex County Greenbelt at (978) 768-7241*

MilesDirections

0.0 START from the gate along a nice, wide doubletrack, heading west, away from Middleton Road. A slight incline quickly runs into a fast descent.

0.2 You'll see what looks to be a camping area to the left. Stay straight, crossing a gravel mound that covers a feeder stream.

0.3 As you pedal, you'll notice a small creek to your left, and several large logs that cross the stream to a parallel trail on the opposite side. Cross this stream, but watch your step. Once on the opposite side, you'll notice that the riding immediately gets more technical, with large exposed roots and sharp rocks. The trail is sandwiched between the creek (which is now on your right) and a small hillside (on your left). Stay on this main trail, ignoring the smaller singletrack trails shooting up the hillside (unless, of course, you want to explore).

0.5 You'll come to a long, loose climb. Make sure you're in the granny gear.

0.6 Another tempting singletrack flies off to the left. Stay on the main trail. The singletrack picks up some speed here.

0.7 Cross over a stone wall.

0.8 Be aware of a quick right turn that takes you right into a short but steep roll-up.

0.9 Come through a wonderful little clearing that's carpeted with pine needles (though a number of rocks are scattered along the trail). The last portion of this section gets quite rocky—a good test of your technical skills.

1.2 Pop back out onto the doubletrack trail. At the "T" intersection, turn left and begin the climb up Bald Hill. You'll see the white blazes here signifying the Bay Circuit Trail. Shortly after you begin you climb, you'll see a well-defined intersection, and you'll want to turn right (again, heading uphill). This juncture is marked by a blue triangle and a trail intersection marker, No. 12.

1.6 Arrive at the top of Bald Hill. You're surrounded by scrub, as well as nice views of the surrounding area. You'll come to a wide intersection, and you'll want to turn left. Be prepared to soak up some bumps as the trail

heads downhill.

1.7 Near the bottom of your descent, you'll see the remnants of the Russell-Hooper farmhouse on your right. Here, our loop bends sharply left before hitting an immediate right (continuing downhill), followed by another quick right at trail juncture No. 10.

2.0 You'll see trail juncture No. 9 going off to the left. This footpath goes through some swampy areas into Middleton, and rarely makes for good riding. Again, this trail features classic New England riding, with lots of loose rocks and big roots.

2.1 You'll see a sign for trail juncture No. 8A. Ignore it, and stay straight.

2.4 Come to a great little water crossing. For those who would rather walk, there's a footbridge to the right. For those who want to ride, stay to the left side and keep your speed up. Momentum is your friend here, especially since the trail goes directly into a tricky, technical climb.

2.8 Reach a big marshy area. The doubletrack is clearly marked, but is typically very wet.

2.9 You'll see trail juncture No. 8 going off to the right. Stay straight, following a blue triangle. (You're now crossing into North Andover.)

3.4 Another creek crossing, with a broken outfall pipe. Ride over the pipe, instead of to the left—a sinkhole here has grabbed many front wheels over the years.

3.5 Come to a trail intersection, marked by two unmistakable landmarks, a pair of bullet-riddled car chassises. Go right here. Just past the car wrecks, come to a big "Y" intersection. Stay to the left, on a trail marked No. 2. This sandy area shortly flows into an open quarry area, an old Nike missile site. The trees are short, and the ground is covered in loose rock. Bear left at the "Y" intersection.

3.6 Take your first right as the trail veers toward the quarry.

3.7 At two big boulders, with the quarry pond in front of you, you'll see a "T" intersection. Go right. Within a few feet, you'll see a shortcut veering off to the right. You can take this if you

MilesDirections

want to try the sharp climb at the other end. If not, just take the main trail.

3.9 After a few fun, steep whoop-dee-dos, you come to the opposite side of the lake into a dirt road. Veer quickly off to the right, on a wide but rocky trail.

4.1 You'll see a trail come in from the right. Ignore it.

4.4 At a "Y" intersection, go right. This is a fun, fast doubletrack.

4.6 Ignore the older trail that shoots off to the left.

4.9 You enter a clearing and come to a "T" intersection—a great place to regroup and grab a drink of water. Go right.

5.2 Take a quick left into a short strip of singletrack.

5.4 Pop out into an intersection, and bear left. If this intersection looks familiar, it is the one portion on our loop that overlaps. Take your first left. This is real rock garden riding.

5.8 Take a sharp right turn, up a short steep hill. This is a choice piece of singletrack, with enough logs and roots to test the most skilled riders.

6.5 Take a right at a subtle "Y" intersection and follow a beautiful singletrack with a high pine canopy that the locals call British Columbia.

6.6 Funnel back into the main trail, staying right.

6.8 At trail intersection, go left.

7.3 Ignore the trail coming in from the left.

7.5 There's another sharp right, going up another sharp incline. Take this trail, marked juncture No. 19. This shortcut spills into a "T" intersection at mile 7.6. Go left here.

7.7 Come to another trail juncture. If you're tired, and you prefer to get to the main road (Middleton Road), stay straight here, and then take a right to get back to the parking area. Otherwise, take a right at trail juncture No. 20A.

7.9 Encounter one of the few lengthy hills. This climb follows a sharp right turn, so gear down beforehand.

8.1 Come to a challenging bridge crossing that's seen its share of endos. Take a left after the footbridge.

8.2 You'll see a sign for trail juncture No. 23 to the right. Ignore it and stay left on the main trail.

8.4 Take a sharp left at trail juncture No. 24.

8.5 Saving the best for last, the trail splits here, and you want to go left, heading downhill. Holler to your heart's content.

8.8 Ignore the trail coming in from the left.

8.9 Check your speed before you burst back out onto Middleton Road. Go right.

9.2 Arrive back at the parking lot, which is now on the right. Regroup, and share stories about your favorite part of the ride.

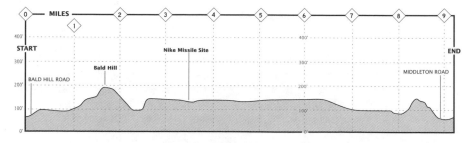

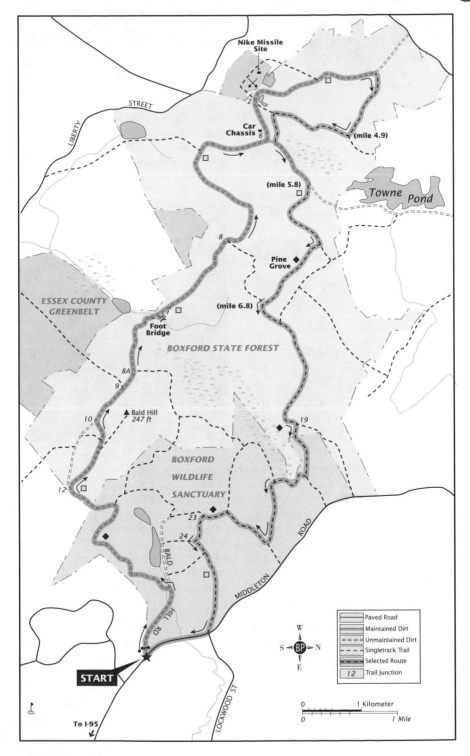

Nike Missile Site

STREET

LIBERTY

Car Chassis 6

(mile 4.9)

(mile 5.8)

Towne Pond

8

Pine Grove

(mile 6.8)

ESSEX COUNTY GREENBELT

Foot Bridge

BOXFORD STATE FOREST

8A

9

10 ▲ Bald Hill 247 ft

19

12

BOXFORD WILDLIFE SANCTUARY

23

24

ROAD

MIDDLETON

BALD

HILL RD

START

To I-95

LOCKWOOD ST

W
N
S ◆ BP ◆ E

	Paved Road
	Maintained Dirt
	Unmaintained Dirt
	Singletrack Trail
	Selected Route
12	Trail Junction

0   1 Kilometer

0   1 Mile

Harold Parker State Forest

Ride Specs

Start: From the trailhead on the right as you enter the park, 0.03 miles from Massachusetts 114

Length: 5.9-mile loop

Approximate Riding Time: 1–1½ hours

Difficulty Rating: Moderate because of the somewhat technical singletrack. Otherwise it's fairly easy to navigate the gentle rolling terrain as there are very few steep climbs and descents.

Terrain: Mainly singletrack with some double-track fire roads and a section of paved road

Elevation Gain: 97 feet

Nearest Town: Andover, MA

Other Trail Users: Hikers and equestrians

Getting There

From Boston: Take I-93 North to I-95 North. Continue on I-95 until MA 114. Take MA 114 west toward Lawrence. The forest entrance is a few miles past Middleton, on the left-hand side of MA 114, marked by two stone pillars and a very visible state forest sign. Turn left here onto Harold Parker Road and park.

DeLorme: Massachusetts Atlas & Gazetteer. Page 29, H-22

Harold Parker State Forest has about 3,500 acres of land for biking, camping, hiking, horseback riding, and many other recreational activities. Within this tract are over 35 miles of trails—and this number is still growing. When this ride was mapped, there were a number of new singletrack paths not yet included on the official state forest trail map. So always be on the lookout for new trails.

Established as a state forest in the early 1900s, Harold Parker State Forest was transformed into a prime recreation area by the Civilian Conservation Corps (CCC). Part of President Franklin Roosevelt's New Deal program to jumpstart the American economy, the CCC provided employment for out-of-work, physically fit, unmarried men between the ages of 18 and 25. Before it was dissolved, the corps had constructed 41,000 bridges, 3,982,000 dams, 44,475 buildings, and applied soil conservation techniques to four million acres in 31 states. Thanks to the CCC, Harold Parker State Forest has an excellent access road system, numerous campsites, and many ponds.

The park affords recreationalists 130 campsites to chose from, a number of good fishing areas, and an ideal location to swim at Berry Pond. If you kayak or have a canoe, the ponds in the forest offer a gentle aquatic workout. Hunting is allowed here, as it is in many Massachusetts state parks, so stop at forest headquarters or call first to find out if hunters will be strolling in the woods during your visit.

This ride takes you through thick stands of oak, maple, and birch trees and down wide horse paths where the views of the foliage are fantastic. The peak season for viewing the changing of the leaves is generally between the middle of October and early November. Most of the ride, because of the number of trees in the forest, is well protected from the wind; so winter rides are feasible as long as there's no snow on the ground. During the snow season, the trails are reserved for cross-country skiers.

Harold Parker State Forest is a fun place to ride without too many hard hills or dangerous descents. And with all the other things it has to offer it's a great place to visit. This forest is fairly close to two other rides in this book which offer, respectively, an easier and a harder ride. They are Bradley Palmer State Park [see Ride 7] and Georgetown Rowley State Forest [see Ride 10].

Ride Information

🍋 Trail Contacts:
Harold Parker State Forest, N. Andover, MA (978) 686-3391 • NEMBA, Action, MA 1-800-57-NEMBA or www.nemba.org

🕐 Schedule:
The park is open year-round. Park officials ask mountain bikers to be respectful of cross-country skiers when there is a layer of snow on the trails.

❓ Local Information:
Merrimack Valley Chamber of Commerce, North Andover, MA (978) 686-0900

🍋 Local Events/Attractions:
Addison Gallery of American Art (1700s to present), at Phillips Academy, Andover, MA (978) 749-4015 • Andover Historical Society, Andover, MA (978) 475-2236

🚲 Local Bike Shops:
Western Cycle, Danvers, MA (987) 774-1685 • Pro Cycles, North Reading, MA (978) 664-9762

Ⓝ Maps:
USGS maps: Reading, MA • Forest maps are available at Forest Headquarters on Middleton Road, (978) 686-3391.

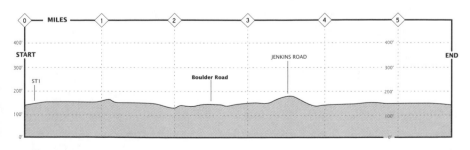

MilesDirections

*[**Note.** Very few of the singletrack trails are marked, although some parts of the trail now have white reflectors to guide riders.]*

0.0 START at the intersection of Harold Parker Road and MA 114 in North Andover. Ride into the park on Harold Parker Road.

0.05 Take a right onto ST1 at the "V"-shaped tree, which is fronted by a small dirt parking area This singletrack trail climbs uphill away from the road.

0.4 Take a left at the "Y" in the trail, continuing on ST1. Pedal up a challenging hill.

0.6 At the stone wall, circle around to the right and continue on ST1.

0.7 At the "T" intersection, take a right onto ST2, a smoother section of singletrack.

1.1 Take a left onto ST3, the intersecting singletrack trail.

1.4 At the "T" intersection, go left on the Mountain Bike Trail. White reflectors will make a sporadic appearance from here on in.

2.4 Cross a dirt fire road (Boulder Road) and go left on Mountain Bike Trail.

2.5 Continue straight on Mountain Bike Trail at this 6-way intersection.

2.6 The trail heads downhill. Go right onto ST4 at the 4-way intersection at the bottom.

2.7 Take a right on Middleton Road—only for a moment.

2.75 Take a left onto Mountain Bike Trail at the tree with four white reflectors on it.

2.9 At the tree that has two reflectors, go right onto ST5.

3.1 Remain to the right on ST5 through two successive "Y" intersections. Then remain on ST5 until it ends at a paved road (Jenkins Road).

3.3 Cross over paved Jenkins Road and enter the forest on Mini Loop 1 at a tree with a white reflector.

3.4 Mini Loop 1 ends at a clearing. Take a right through the clearing back to Jenkins Road.

3.45 Take a left onto Jenkins Road.

3.7 Take a right onto paved Middleton Road.

4.0 Take a right onto Rec Road 1 into the Berry Pond Recreation Area.

4.2 Turn around and head back out to Middleton Road.

4.3 Take a right onto Middleton Road.

4.8 Take a left into the forest on DT1 at the obvious doubletrack trail between two trees.

5.1 Follow DT1 as it winds to the right.

5.5 Emerge onto Harold Parker Road and take a left.

5.9 End the ride at the dirt parking area on the left where you first entered the forest on ST1.

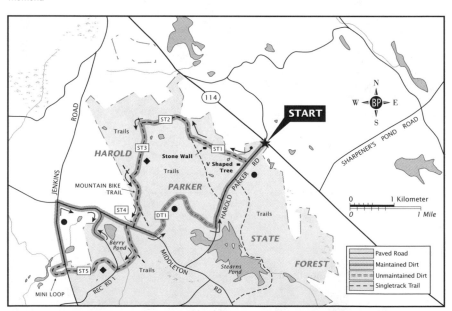

Dogtown Common

Ride Specs

Start: From the parking area on Dogtown Road
Length: 10.7-mile circuit
Approximate Riding Time: 2–2½ hours
Difficulty Rating: Moderate to difficult because of the amount of technical riding. Climbs and descents are only difficult because of the terrain. The grades are not too tough.
Terrain: Doubletrack fire roads covered with small rocks, dirt fire roads, technical singletrack. This is a fairly dry ride and the only perpetually wet areas are at the stone dam and on some lower doubletrack roads.
Elevation Gain: 484 feet
Nearest Town: Gloucester, MA
Other Trail Users: Hikers and equestrians

Getting There

From Boston: Travel north on I-93 to MA 128 East (Exit 37). Take MA 128 to Gloucester. Reach the rotary at MA 127. Follow MA 127 to Poplar Street, and take a right on Poplar.

Follow to Cherry Street on the left. Take Cherry Street a short distance until you reach Dogtown Road. Take a right onto Dogtown Road, and park in the lot by the Common map.
DeLorme: Massachusetts Atlas & Gazetteer. Page 30, H-15

Via Ferry (Summer Only): Take the Gloucester Ferry to Gloucester. Now on your bike, proceed north on Washington Street, cross the MBTA tracks, and make a right on Derby Street. Turn left on Maplewood Street, cross under MA 128, and take a left onto Poplar. Take a right on Cherry Street and another right onto Dogtown Road. Park in the lot by the Common map. For more information, call A.C. Cruise Lines at 1-800-422-8419.

Via the Ⓣ: Take the MBTA Rockport line to Gloucester Station at Washington Street and Railroad Avenue. Head north on Washington Street and follow the ferry directions above.

Dogtown Common was named for the packs of wild dogs that roamed the streets in the early 1800s. The town had become a haven for the destitute when the rich pulled up stakes and moved to the coast. The less prosperous remained behind and soon were practicing prostitution and living in squalor. The last resident of Dogtown was relocated to the poor house in the 1830s, and the town was abandoned. Then entered the wild dogs.

Eventually the canine population died off and today the only thing resembling a dog in this fun park are the numerous rocks ranging in size from a Chihuahua to a Great Dane. By the time I finished mapping this ride I was calling it "Rocktown" Common. But this ride offers more than just technical sections. The fast doubletrack sections on the western side of the park allow you to remain in your middle ring for long stretches of time. And for a diversion, there's good fishing to be had by Babson Reservoir.

Cruising through this abandoned town of dogs can do more than pump up your thighs; it can also inspire you. In many locations throughout the park there are boulders with sayings carved into them. These messages, such as "Keep Out Of Debt," "Study," "Integrity," and "Ideas," were commissioned by a well-intentioned Gloucester native, Roger Babson, in the 1930s. After hearing how the residents of Dogtown met their fate, Babson took it upon himself to inspire those who wandered through the historic town. Now the paths have about two dozen inspirational and directional messages, as well as about 40 small rocks with numbers on them to mark where houses in Dogtown once stood before they were razed.

These aren't the only rocks present on the trails. The doubletrack fire roads are littered with loose, fist-sized stones that make riding a little treacherous and handling the bike quite frightening. There are also medium-sized boulders that cover the trail that descends to the Babson Reservoir. On this ride you travel this route down and then back up to provide more of a challenge. And finally, the gravel found near the Goose Cove Reservoir and on the doubletrack leading down to the water is somewhat hard to climb but doesn't prove too difficult when going downhill.

The trails in Dogtown offer a mix of challenging, rocky terrain and smooth, fast doubletrack roads. Riders will find that the trails are often not crowded and the assorted scenery (overlooking Babson Reservoir and peering through the woods in the northern part of the park) can help calm the nerves of even the most frazzled city dweller.

Today Dogtown Common is owned by the towns of Gloucester and Rockport and has a vast network of public trails within it. A byproduct of this co-ownership is that the land is well protected and will probably never see houses built on it again.

Ride Information

🟢 Trail Contacts:
Cape Ann Chamber of Commerce, Gloucester, MA (978) 283-1601 • **NEMBA,** Action, MA 1-800-57-NEMBA or www.nemba.org

🕐 Schedule:
Riding is open year-round, but the Common is frequently closed during high forest fire risk times. Call the Cape Ann Chamber of Commerce or the Gloucester Fire Department to find out if the park is open.

❓ Local Information:
Cape Ann Chamber of Commerce, Gloucester, MA (978) 283-1601 • **Cape Ann Whale Watch**, Gloucester, MA (978) 283-5110 • **Seven Seas Whale Watch**, Gloucester, MA (978) 283-1776 • **Yankee Fleet Whale Watch**, Gloucester, MA (978) 283-0313

📍 Local Events/Attractions:
St. Peter's Fiesta, last weekend in June, Gloucester, MA – *a blessing of the fleet and fireworks festival* • Local beaches, Gloucester, MA – *are crowded, yet beautiful from June through September*

🚴 Local Bike Shops:
Aries Sports & Bikery, Newbury, MA (978) 465-8099 • **Bay Road Bikes**, South Hamilton, MA (978) 468-1301 • **National Bike Shop**, Beverly, MA (978) 922-8215

Ⓝ Maps:
USGS maps: Rockport, MA • Maps cost $2 and are available from the Cape Ann Chamber of Commerce, (978) 283-1601. A map is displayed in the parking lot.

MilesDirections

0.0 START at the fire gate at the end of the entrance on Dogtown Road.

0.2 Continue straight on the doubletrack fire road through the second fire gate.

0.6 At reflector #1, take a left into the woods on the singletrack Adams Pines Trail.

0.8 Go left at the split in the trail, remaining on the main trail.

1.1 Take a right at the "T" intersection on the doubletrack Common Road.

1.6 At reflector #5, take a right onto the singletrack Wharf Road.

1.9 Take a left at the "Y" intersection with a doubletrack Dogtown Road.

2.0 Take a left onto a short singletrack trail TR1. "Get Out Of Debt" is on the rock on this trail.

2.1 Turn around at the rock and return to the doubletrack Dogtown Road and take a left.

2.2 At reflector #8, take a right onto the singletrack Babson Boulder Trail. Follow this trail straight to the bottom.

2.8 Go straight across the sand at the end of the trail onto the large boulder at the edge of the reservoir.

2.9 Turn around at the top of the boulder and head back up the Babson Boulder Trail.

3.5 At the clearing bear to the right onto TR2, and head toward the huge rock. Follow TR2 across the field.

3.7 Take a left onto Dogtown Road.

4.0 At reflector #1, take a right onto Adams Pines Trail.

4.4 Go left at the "T" intersection with DT1, a doubletrack fire road.

4.5 Take a right onto the doubletrack service road SR1, which surrounds Goose Cove Reservoir. Follow SR1 all the way around to the fire road at reflector #3.

6.5 At reflector #3, take a right onto Common Road.

6.9 Turn right onto the singletrack Wharf Road Extension, at reflector #4.

7.0 Take a left at the "T" intersection onto Wharf Road.

7.2 Go right onto Common Road, a doubletrack, dirt fire road.

7.9 At the "Y" in the trail, go right onto Luce Trail. Soon the trail crosses over a cement dam.

8.2 Take a hairpin left at the end of the dam, still on Luce Trail. The trail winds over a wooden bridge and back to the doubletrack fire road Common Road.

8.3 Take a right onto Common Road.

9.7 At reflector #2, go left onto Adams Pines Trail and follow to the end.

10.1 Take a right on Dogtown Road, heading toward the parking area.

10.7 Finish the ride at the fire gate at the end of the paved entrance road.

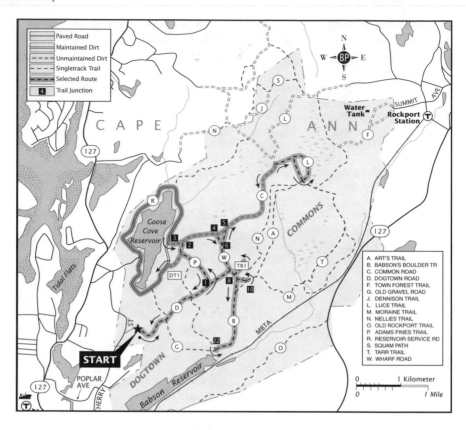

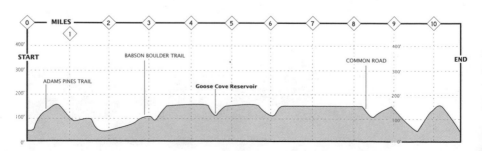

Ravenswood Park

14

Ride Specs

Start: From the parking lot off MA 127
Length: 4.4-mile loop, with options to connect to several additional singletrack trails
Approximate Riding Time: Advanced Riders, 40 minutes; Intermediate Riders, 1 hour
Difficulty Rating: Technically difficult due to occasional rocky sections. Physically moderate due to short mileage and some moderate climbing, plus a fair percentage of technical riding.
Terrain: Hardscrabble; technical singletrack; and smooth, gentle doubletrack. Depending on the trail choice, this will be smooth, rolling forestland, haphazard, granite boulder fields with quick climbs and drops, or a combination of both.
Elevation Gain: 126 feet
Nearest Town: Gloucester, MA
Other Trail Users: Hikers, joggers, bird watchers, picnickers, cross-country skiers, and snowshoers

Getting There

From Boston: Take U.S. 1 North to MA 128 East, toward Gloucester. Take the exit for MA 133 East (Exit 14). Follow MA 133 three miles into downtown Gloucester, and to a "T" intersection with MA 127 (Western Avenue). You'll see Gloucester Harbor and the Atlantic Ocean directly in front of you, and the entrance to Stage Fort Park just to the right. Take a right onto MA 127. Ravenswood Park is two miles down the road, on the right side, and marked by a large wooden sign. *DeLorme: Massachusetts Atlas & Gazetteer:* Page 30, J-14

Via the (T): Take the MBTA Rockport line from North Station to West Gloucester Station. Now on your bike, head east from the station on to MA 133. Turn right on to MA 127 (Western Avenue). Ravenswood Park is two miles down the road, on the right side, and marked by a large wooden sign. (Total biking distance from West Gloucester Station to start: 3.1 miles.)

You can look, but it's unlikely you'll find a more challenging collection of singletrack than the rocky paths of Ravenswood Park on the Cape Ann shoreline. The more advanced routes in this 500-acre park mirror New England's rugged coast—rocky ribbons of trail zigzagging through a forest littered with immense, imposing boulders. That's not to say that this refuge doesn't offer something for riders of every ability level. In fact, the carriage paths of Ridge Road and Old Salem Road are wide, well-groomed thoroughfares with gentle pitches, ideal for the beginning mountain bikers. Still, to enjoy all the delights to be found in the 10 miles of trail here, you have to be ready to take your riding to the next level, in both stamina and technical skills. Your efforts will be rewarded tenfold, in terms of your own sense of accomplishment and the sights to be found.

Ravenswood, like the rest of Cape Ann, was once covered in ice. When the glaciers retreated northward, kettles, bogs, and swampland were left behind, not to mention fields of glacial erratics (boulders). The views of Gloucester Harbor are matched by the woodlands, which include red oak, white pine, paper birch, and maple, and shrubs such as huckleberry, low-bush blueberry, mountain laurel, arrowroot, and witch hazel. Local wildflowers include pink lady's slipper, bluebead lily, trailing arbutus, and colonies of ferns. Sightings of red-tailed hawks and great horned owls are not uncommon.

In addition to its natural history, the park boasts a colorful cultural past. In 1884, Mason A. Walton (a.k.a. the "Hermit of Ravenswood Park") moved here to cure himself of tuberculosis. He settled close to Old Salem Road and built a cabin on the north side of the park—a plaque marks the spot. He studied the flora and fauna and wrote several books before his death in 1917. In the second half of the 19th Century, Gloucester-native Samuel Sawyer began purchasing numerous wood lots, old pastures, and swampland around his home on Old Salem Road with the intent of later establishing a park. When he died, in 1889, he left more than 26 parcels of land with an endowment to create Ravenswood, which would "be laid out handsomely with driveways and pleasant rural walks." By 1916, roads and trails had been constructed. For more than a century, the Trustees of Ravenswood Park managed the park before the property was transferred to The Trustees of Reservations in 1993.

The loop described here incorporates all elements of this park, from white-knuckle singletrack to wide-open fire roads. All the difficult sections can be walked, if necessary, so don't be intimidated. Though admittedly challenging, these trails lead you to the best vistas offered in Ravenswood, as well as a newfound appreciation for the art of trail building. If you're content to stay on the fire roads, however, you can put together a nice loop without having to venture on the singletrack at all. Since the singletrack starts rather quickly from you're starting point at the parking lot, you might opt for a fire road spin first simply to warm up.

Also keep in mind that, due to local policy, the Trustees of Reservations do not mark these trails with painted dots or blazes. Occasionally you'll find a trail marker, but they're rare. The benefit of this policy is the preservation of the wilderness "feel" of the reservation. Still, this park is fairly enclosed, and you can find your way back to the main carriage paths without much difficulty.

Ride Information

🕭 Trail Contacts:

Trustees of Reservations, Beverly, MA (978) 921-1944 or www.thetrustees.org • **Ravenswood Superintendent** (978) 281-0041

🕔 Schedule:

May 1 to February 28. Closed to mountain bikes March 1 through April 30 to protect trails during muddy season.

💲 Fees/Permits:

There's no fee, but you must be a Trustees member or have a mountain bike pass. For a mountain bike pass or to become a TOR member, call the general headquarters in Beverly, MA at (978) 921-1944.

🜚 Local Events/Attractions:

Periodic public programs. Consult the "Events & Programs" section of the Trustees of Reservations website at www.thetrustees.org for current listings.

🕭 Local Bike Shops:

Harborside Cycles, Gloucester, MA (978) 281-7744 • **Seaside Cycles,** Manchester-by-the-Sea, MA (978) 526-1200

🅝 Maps:

USGS maps: Gloucester, MA

MilesDirections

0.0 START from the small parking lot (12-car maximum) and pedal west on a smooth, graded carriage path, Old Salem Road.

0.1 Come to a well-marked trail intersection on the right. The sign indicates the Ledge Hill Trail. Immediately this trail begins to show the reservation's (and Cape Ann's) true colors, with numerous chunks of granite popping through the dirt floor.

0.2 Go straight through this subtle trail intersection, veering off the Ledge Hill Trail and onto an unmarked but well-defined hiking trail.

0.4 A trail veers off to the right into adjoining private property. Stay to the left.

0.6 Here the trail becomes very, very challenging—and you'll understand why it's described as a "hiking" trail. Enormous boulders line the trail, and the trail itself becomes a true rock garden that demands your best trials skills. Most people have to hike-a-bike up and over this rocky terrain, so don't be embarrassed to follow suit.

0.8 You spill back onto the Ledge Hill Trail, which is well defined if not well marked. Go left here, and start climbing a short, technical hill to a magnificent vista on your left overlooking the southern Gloucester shoreline (known as Magnolia) and the Atlantic Ocean.

0.9 Note the handiwork of this rolling, rock-lined

corridor, where industrious trail builders made wonderful use of the area's abundant rock to form a curbed singletrack. It's very technical in sections.

1.0 Come to a fork in the trail, and stay right along the rock-lined path.

1.3 You'll see another trail coming in from the left. Stay straight.

1.5 This singletrack flows back into the main carriage path. Go right. On the opposite side of this road, note the sign for the Magnolia Swamp Trail—one of two trails in the park that have been deemed off-limits to mountain bikes. Just up the road the carriage road splits, and you'll veer right onto Ridge Road.

1.7 Take a right onto a narrow singletrack.

1.9 At the top of a steep, short climb, you'll come to a "T" intersection and the Ledge Hill Trail. This is the one section where you'll double back on trails that you've already ridden, but given their technical nature, they're bound to look very different going in the opposite direction. Go left.

2.1 Just before you get back to the vista (mile 0.8), you'll see a trail off to the left. Take it, and be prepared for a loose, gravelly descent with some tight switchbacks.

2.3 This footpath spills back into Ridge Road. Go right and immediately notice the three-way inter-

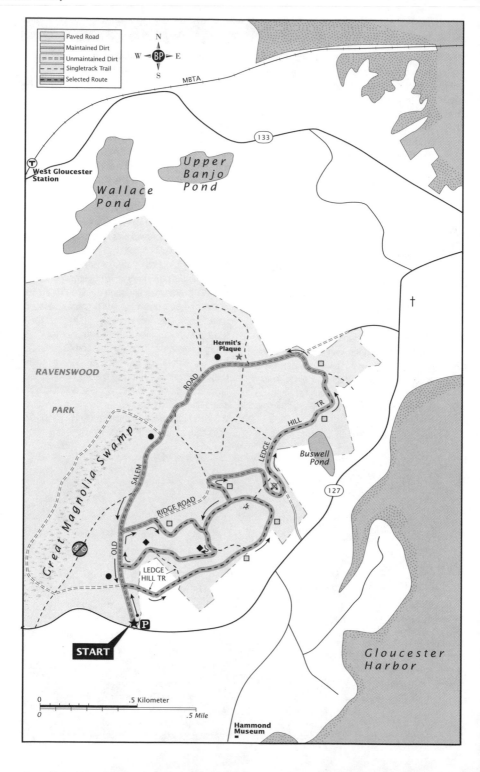

Paved Road
Maintained Dirt
Unmaintained Dirt
Singletrack Trail
Selected Route

N
W — E
S
BP

MBTA

133

West Gloucester
Station

*Upper
Banjo
Pond*

*Wallace
Pond*

RAVENSWOOD

PARK

Hermit's
Plaque

Great Magnolia Swamp

ROAD

SALEM

HILL TR

LEDGE

*Buswell
Pond*

127

RIDGE ROAD

OLD

LEDGE
HILL TR

START

P

0   .5 Kilometer
0   .5 Mile

*Gloucester
Harbor*

Hammond
Museum

MilesDirections *continued*

section. Take the hairpin turn back to the right, which leads us to the remnants of an old quarry.

2.5 On the right, you'll see where the Ledge Hill Trail enters the carriage path on the right. Take this right, and loop around the small water-filled quarry—a vestige of one of the area's earliest industries. This is a great spot to break for lunch. Following the trail around the quarry (keeping it on your left), come back to the carriage road and start heading west again. Almost immediately, you'll come to a singletrack on the right, with a yellow marker. This is the continuation of the Ledge Hill Trail. Take this right.

2.8 Following a couple of hairy hairpin drops, you'll come to a wet area and an iron pipe that crosses the trail. Hop over this wet area, and note the trail to the left. This is another trail closed to mountain bikes, and is typically posted as such. Our loop heads up the hill directly in front of you. It features some tricky switchbacks, so you'll want to have your chain in the granny gear. At the top of this climb, you'll see some narrow singletrack

trails running off to the right. These trails also offer nice overlooks, but they end shortly.

3.1 Come to a "T" intersection, and go left onto a nice, wide doubletrack.

3.3 You'll see a trail coming in from the left with a "no biking" sign. Just past this intersection you'll flow into the main carriage road, Old Salem Road. *[**Option.** To add another stretch of single-track to your ride, look for the trail to the right, by the plaque dedicated to Mason A. Walton, "The Hermit of Ravenswood." This trail loops north, then west and south, eventually hooking back into Old Salem Road. Otherwise, stay on this loop and the wide carriage path.]*

3.7 Ignore the trail coming in from the left and head straight up a short hill.

4.1 You'll complete the carriage path loop, coming back to the intersection where Ridge Road veers off (it will now be on your left). Stay straight and head for the parking lot.

4.4 You're back at your car.

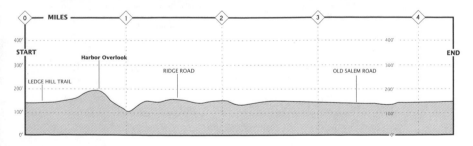

15   Chebacco Woods

Ride Specs

Start: From the main entrance/trailhead off Chebacco Road

Length: 4.8-mile loop, with options to connect to numerous singletrack and doubletrack trails

Approximate Riding Time: Advanced Riders, 40 minutes; Intermediate Riders, 1 hour

Difficulty Rating: Technically easy to moderate due to occasional rocky and/or muddy single-track sections. Physically easy to moderate due to short mileage and some moderate climbing.

Terrain: Singletrack, doubletrack, and some rough dirt roads. Undulating New England topography, with many exposed rocks and roots.

Elevation Gain: 107 feet

Nearest Towns: Hamilton, MA

Other Trail Users: Hikers, joggers, bird watchers, picnickers, equestrians, anglers, cross-country skiers, and snowshoers

Getting There

From Boston: Take U.S. 1 North to MA 128 East, toward Gloucester. Take the exit for MA 22 North to Essex (Exit 18). Follow MA 22 to Hamilton and turn right onto Chebacco Road. At 0.7 miles after you turn onto Chebacco Road, you'll see Chebacco Lake to the left and a small parking area on the right. The main entrance to Chebacco Woods is marked with a painted wooden sign. *DeLorme: Massachusetts Atlas & Gazetteer:* Page 30, I-6

B oston's North Shore enjoys an abundance of postage stamp-sized parcels of woodland, islands of escape in this fairly urban setting. Among these prized retreats is the forest situated behind Gordon College, a small Christian school in Wenham, Massachusetts. Today, the forest represents much more than a wooded sanctuary. It serves as a glowing testament to the power to civic action.

For many years, hikers, runners, cross-country skiers and mountain bikers enjoyed unfettered access to this inviting labyrinth of trails. But by the mid 1990s, the college began marketing a huge section of this valuable forest. Many feared the land would be developed for housing, and thus a rare resource, and an integral link in the ring of undeveloped land stretching from West Gloucester to Beverly, would be lost forever.

Galvanized by the potential loss of this wooded jewel, and aided by state grants and an incredibly generous offer from an anonymous benefactor to match all private donations, residents from the towns of Hamilton and Manchester-by-the-Sea joined hands by raising more than $300,000 to buy 113 acres in 1998. Combined with the 250-acre drinking water supply land owned by Manchester-by-the-Sea, Chebacco Woods today covers 363 acres of prime wildlife habitat, and prime trail riding terrain. Though situated only 25 miles north of Boston, alongside the Technology Highway (Massachusetts 128), the dense deciduous and evergreen forest creates a natural buffer from noise. The

solitude and stillness found here is remarkably similar to that found in the wilderness areas of Maine, New Hampshire, and Vermont. Though you might hear gunfire coming from the other side of Chebacco Road, there is no hunting on this property. What you're hearing is the nearby Hamilton Rod and Gun Club.

There are also many unpublished routes that split from the main trails on the Chebacco Woods Trail Map, many of which offer some of the area's best technical riding, and some which drop right in behind the campus of Gordon College on Grapevine Road. Leave yourself some extra time to explore these subtle routes. Also, dog owners should know that Gravelly and Round ponds comprise the drinking water supply for Manchester-by-the-Sea, and so dogs are not allowed in these waters. Dogs are, however welcome on all upland portions of Chebacco Woods.

Ride Information

🕯 Trail Contacts:
Chebacco Woods Land Management Committee, Hamilton Conservation Commission (978) 468-5583 • Manchester Conservation Commission (978) 526-4397

🕐 Schedule:
Year-round, half-hour before sunrise to half-hour after sunset

🍴 Restaurants:
Weathervane Tavern, Hamilton MA (978) 468-2600 • 7 Central Publick House, Manchester-by-the-Sea, MA (978) 526-7494

🚲 Local Bike Shops:
Seaside Cycles, Manchester-by-the-Sea, MA (978) 526-1200 • Bay Road Bikes, Railroad Avenue, Hamilton, MA (978) 468-1301

🅽 Maps:
USGS maps: Salem, MA • Chebacco Woods Trail Map, Chebacco Woods Land Management Committee – available at the town halls and town libraries of Hamilton and Manchester-by-the-Sea

MilesDirections

0.0 START with Chebacco Lake at your back. Head south onto the main trail, marked by the carved Chebacco Woods sign. Shortly after the entrance is a chain (usually marked with pink streamers) running across the trail, ostensibly to keep out unauthorized motorized vehicles. Be aware of this chain, especially if you're riding during low light. Just past the chain is a sign posting on the right side of the trail welcoming you to Chebacco Woods, with a detailed map of the main trail in the area.

0.1 After a slight rise, you'll come to a trail intersection, with a sign White to Red Connector straight in front of you, and Round Pond behind that. Keep this intersection in mind, since our loop will finish here. Go right.

0.2 On your right is a narrow strip of single-track that leads to a very technical route known by the locals as the House Trail (named so because it runs to the back of the trail builder's house on Chebacco Road). Stay straight, though, and take your first left just past this spot, onto the Red Dot Trail. This stretch is fairly rocky to start, and very rooty as you get closer to Coy Pond in Wenham.

0.7 After a quick descent, come to a "T" intersection, with Coy Pond directly in front of you and Gordon College behind the pond. Go left. [*Option.* A right turn here will allow you to skirt around the pond and eventually reconnect with our loop by Gull Pond.] As you pedal toward Gull Pond, you'll see several trails springing off to the left. Ignore them.

0.9 Stay on the main trail as it bends to the right and crosses a feeder stream.

1.0 Come into a clearing with a gravel road. Bear left and then right at Gull Pond. You'll see a small beach in front of you—a great place to cool off near the end of our ride. Continue on, keeping Gull Pond on your left.

1.2 At a four-way intersection, continue straight across while bearing left. (A sharp left here will keep you along the pond, while a right brings you to Gordon College.)

1.3 Take a well-defined right turn, which leads to a terrific little section known as The Birches.

Shortly after the right, you'll see a singletrack trail heading up to the left. Take it onto a pair of short, loose rocky climbs.

1.4 The trail drops into a grove of birch trees that runs alongside Massachusetts 128—urban mountain biking at its best.

1.5 At a T-intersection, bear left. *[Option. You can go right here, since the loops reconnect later. This route features a large, granite outcropping that only the most talented bike handlers can clean, and you might want to see how you measure up.]* Otherwise, go left and look for a sharp right turn in the next 20 yards.

1.6 Again, you are heading toward Massachusetts 128. You'll see where the other shortcut connects in from the right. Go left onto a loose rocky drop, and follow this singletrack back onto the wide doubletrack.

1.7 When you pop back onto the doubletrack, go right.

1.8 *[Option. You'll see a trail on the right side that cuts sharply upward into a hillside. This is the beginner of Shiftlever, an enticing slice of singletrack favored by local riders. It's roughly a mile-and-a-half long, and very challenging. It eventually pops out onto Pine Street in Manchester-by-the-Sea (which is the same road as Chebacco Road in Hamilton). If you take this route, go left onto Pine Street and pedal back to the access road you're on now, about a half mile.]* For this loop, we'll stay straight here, ignoring the trail to the left just past the shift lever entrance.

1.9 You'll see another trail that hairpins to your left. You have two options here. Beginner riders will want to take this first left onto a level trail. More advanced riders will want to take the second left, which pops over a small hill and affords some very technical obstacles. The cues here follow the advanced option.

2.0 The technical trail spills back into the beginner trail. You'll take a quick right, followed by another right at the bottom of the hill. Within several yards, you'll take a left, over a rough log footbridge that crosses some wetlands, and then strike into a rooty climb.

MilesDirections *continued*

2.2 Come to another "Y" intersection, where riders of varying abilities have a choice. The right trail is more beginner-oriented, while the left, though not extreme, has some interesting drops. We're going left here.

2.3 At the bottom of a narrow descent, you'll see the other trail connecting from the right. Go left here and follow this trail up and around a little knoll before dropping into a well-groomed doubletrack.

2.4 At that doubletrack, take a right, and

almost immediately take a left down a loose gravel access road. At this last intersection, you'll see Gravelly Pond in front of you, as well as the Manchester Water Treatment Plant, and a small sign pointing right—this simply leads you out of the woods and onto Chebacco Road. Ignore the sign and go left, dropping into an earthen esker and followed by a moderate, looping climb.

2.6 At a trail juncture, the main singletrack veers left. You'll want to take the trail less trav-

MilesDirections *continued*

eled (to the right), onto a narrow, bouncy section—again, you'll see Gravelly Pond to your right. This trail finishes with a steep, rutted descent, so be aware.

2.7 At the bottom of that drop, sweep to the left and come to another trail intersection. *[Option. A right here puts you on the Yellow Dot Trail, a rooty section that continues between Round and Gravelly ponds and eventually punches out onto Chebacco Road near Hamilton's public beach on Chebacco Lake. You can also go straight, but this path along Round Pond tends to be wet most of the year.]* We're turning left, back up the hill.

2.8 At the "T" Intersection, take a right and another almost immediate right.

2.9 You'll see a trail veering off to the right, marked by a few old rusty triangles. This flows into a quick downhill and then up to a knoll that overlooks Round Pond. You'll want to keep your momentum high for the sharp climb at the bottom.

3.0 Bear left at the pond and follow the trail that hugs the hillside.

3.1 Halfway around this mound, bear right (again blazed with yellow markers).

3.3 You'll see the main trail flow back in from the left. Continue straight.

3.4 Ignore the small trail off to the right. Just past this, at the top of a short rise, is another right that splits from the main trail. Take this right. This narrow route features a quick drop that funnels into a nice S-turn, so you want to be prepared.

3.6 Come to a "T" intersection. Take a left and almost an immediate right at a "T" intersection, where you'll see Gull Pond in front of you. *[Option. You may also notice a hairpin right here, which leads to a poorly maintained but challenging trail that winds through a muddy section of the woods. I don't recommend it, but some riders can't resist getting muddy.]* You'll come in to the pond and the public beach that we passed earlier. If it's a hot day, there's no better place to cool off. Go straight after the sandy section along the Yellow-Red Connector Trail.

3.8 Take a right, doubling back on the gravel trail we came out on earlier.

3.9 At this "Y" intersection, you'll stay right (marked by a red square), hugging the shore of Round Pond. This trail has some sharp corners, and you should be aware of other trail users here.

4.0 You'll see a trail to the right, which is the other end of the wet trail mentioned at mile 3.6.

4.4 At the White-Red Connector, bear left, up a small incline, and head back to the main intersection where this loop began. At the main four-way intersection, you can head straight across and back to your car. For one last section of singletrack, go right here.

4.6 This singletrack finishes with a very sharp, off-camber drop that funnels onto Chebacco Road. If you have any doubts about your bike-handling ability, walk it. At the bottom, take a left onto Chebacco Road, and head to the parking area.

4.8 Arrive back at your car and the main entrance to Chebacco Woods.

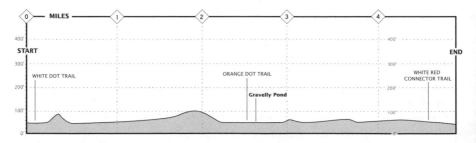

90

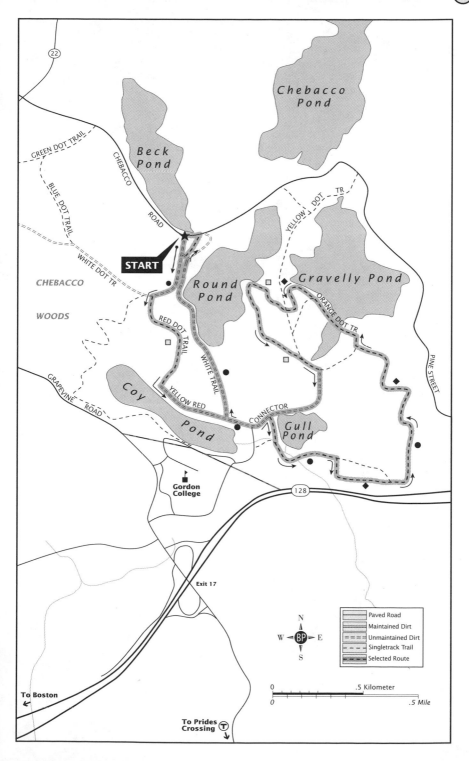

South of Boston

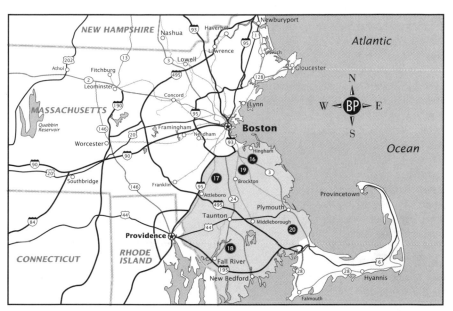

The region south of Boston includes the South Shore and many communities that are not on the water but are fairly close to it. The riding here, like in the city itself, can be enjoyed nearly year-round. There are certainly times when riding outside is inadvisable—during blizzards for example—but for the most part, trails are rideable throughout the seasons.

When you head south of Boston you'll notice the landscape beginning to change slightly. The cover from birch, oak, and maple trees becomes thicker than you'll find in any of the regions featured in this guide. There are also many pine trees down here, and in the fall the trails become covered with their cushiony needles—much more so than up north where the trails are primarily covered in hardwood leaves.

As far as the trails are concerned, you'll find more rocks and roots on the trails. One South ride in particular, Borderland, is a smorgasbord of different size rocks for 75 percent of the trail. Suspension on that trail is highly recommended. Another element of this landscape is sand, especially as the South rides move toward Plymouth. Overall, the South offers a variety of trails for short and long rides by the water or slightly inland.

16

Wompatuck State Park

Ride Specs

Start: From the last fire gate on the right, at the back of the park

Length: 9.6-mile circuit

Approximate Riding Time: 1–1½ hours

Difficulty Rating: Moderate—beginners may have difficulty with some of the terrain and obstructions

Terrain: Paved fire roads, doubletrack, and singletrack—abundant roots and loose rocks, some soft base, and moderate amount of packed dirt

Elevation Gain: 328 feet

Nearest Town: Hingham, MA

Other Trail Users: Hikers, equestrians, and cross-country skiers

Getting There

From Boston: Take I-93 South to the Braintree / MA 3 exchange. Take MA 3 South toward Cape Cod. Take Exit 14 (MA 228—Hingham) and take a left at the bottom of the ramp. Follow MA 228 (Main Street in Hingham) straight for about four miles until you see High Street on your right,

next to the South Shore Baptist Church. There will also be a small sign for Wompatuck State Park on your right. Take a right on High Street and follow it until you see the entrance to Wompatuck State Park on your right. Drive exactly two miles and park at the fire gate on the right. Do not block the fire gate or your car will be gone when you return. *DeLorme: Massachusetts Atlas & Gazetteer.* Page 54, C-5

Though weather can be harsh at certain times of the years, riding in Coastal Massachusetts and in the seaside community of Hingham can be done almost year-round with the correct gear and clothing. Some items you will want to take along for the ride are bug spray, water, and a windbreaker in case the breeze picks up. On occasion the mosquitoes can be vicious.

This ride was developed on the route of a race that took place in the park during the summer of 1996. The race has since moved on, giving this trail a chance to recover. This resting period hasn't restored all the damage racers caused, and you should expect numerous puddles and an abundance of protruding rocks and roots. These features and the variety of terrain will challenge most abilities. Finding the correct tire pressure is a challenge as the terrain varies drastically. In some areas you'll slog through loose sand and have a need for soft tires, but the trail can change quickly to rocky dropoffs that will pinch flat most tires in the blink of an eye. Keep tires between 38 and 48 psi for most conditions here. In addition, suspension is nice to have while cruising over the roots and rocks, but it can become cumbersome when trying to wend your way up the hills and between the countless wind-downed trees.

If you get hungry after your ride, or just want to take in the scenery and history of nearby Hingham, take a right out of the park and follow the road past the high school straight into the downtown area. As with most rides in this guide, there is more to see than just the dirt.

The town of Hingham is an affluent, seaside community of nearly 30,000 people, located 12 miles south of Boston. Taking it's name from its sister town in England, Hingham was one of the first incorporated towns in the region (1635), and though it may be overshadowed by its neighbors—Quincy, Plymouth, and Boston—Hingham can claim an honor none of those other towns can. Eleanor Roosevelt once honored the community by saying that Hingham's Main Street was one of the most beautiful streets in America.

On your way to Wompatuck State Park look at the houses that line Main Street, the majority of which are from the 18th Century. Conservative in color and decoration, these homes are kept in top shape. In fact, there exists an unspoken rule that houses along Main Street are to remain this way. A few years back a furor arose when one Main Street resident dared to break with tradition and display colored lights during the holiday season—instead of the more "respectable" white variety. There were editorials in the local papers denouncing the evil deed. Not much else was done about the indiscretion, but most residents still conform to the "all-white lights" rule.

Ride Information

📞 Trail Contacts:
Wompatuck State Park: (781) 749-7160 • **NEMBA,** Action, MA 1-800-57-NEMBA or *www.nemba.org*

🕐 Schedule:
The park is open year-round but only has daylight visiting hours.

❓ Local Information:
Division of Fisheries & Wildlife, Boston, MA (617) 727-3151. • **Hingham Town Clerk's Office,** Hingham, MA (781) 741-1410 •**Boston Harbor Islands State Park,** Boston, MA (617) 727-7676

📍 Local Events/Attractions:
Hingham holds a footrace down Main Street each 4TH of July • **Christmas in the Square,** Hingham, MA – *local merchants serve eggnog and baked treats and the downtown streets are closed off for Santa to arrive in a fire engine*

🛏 Accommodations:
There is a campground inside the park and camping is allowed only during the spring and summer months. RV hookups and sanitary facilities are available for campers.

🍴 Restaurants:
Atlantic Bagel & Coffee, Hingham, MA (781) 740-0636 • **Stars Restaurant,** Hingham, MA (781) 749-3200 • **Liberty Grille,** Hingham, MA (781) 749-2444

🚲 Local Bike Shops:
Harbor Cycles, Hingham, MA (781) 749-1077 • **The Bicycle Link,** Weymouth, MA (781) 337-7125 • **Quincy Cycle,** Quincy, MA (617) 471-2321

🅝 Maps:
USGS MAPS: Weymouth, MA • Maps of the park are available at park headquarters at the front of the park, (781) 749-7160.

The Hingham area has more than its architecture and manners rooted in the past. Its surroundings are constant reminders of history. The Old Ship Church in Hingham Center was built in 1681 and is the oldest church structure to have been used continuously for worship in the United States. Just outside of Hingham Harbor sits George's Island, a 30-acre island that's home to Fort Warren. This military fort, built between 1833 and 1869 out of granite, was used as a training facility during the Civil War and later as a prison for captured Confederates. It's a fantastic place to picnic on sunny summer days. You can take a ferry from Boston to visit this and other harbor islands for a reasonable charge. War-buffs might note that throughout Wompatuck State Park are bunkers, now mostly filled with dirt, that served as storage units for U.S. munitions, vehicles, and other supplies in both World Wars.

These days the only munitions allowed near Hingham are those used by local hunters. That's when riding can become dangerous—that is, if it weren't for our religious forefathers. In their infinite wisdom, they saw fit to legally prohibited work on Sundays—these same laws, so-called "Blue Laws," outlaw hunting on Sundays. So, when riding in Massachusetts, if you're not sure whether hunting season is in or out, take your bike to the trail on a Sunday just to be safe.

ALERT!
Don't cut new trails at Wompatuck State Forest!

The land manager at Wompatuck State Forest has asked NEMBA to urge the mountain bikers cutting renegade trails in his park to stop immediately!

A few new unauthorized trails are being built in Wompatuck State Forest without permission and while the individuals responsible may feel that they are doing a service to the park, the opposite is the case, and it could jeopardize the good relations that mountain bikers currently enjoy in this park. State forest personnel consider unauthorized trail construction to be vandalism.

Please let all bikers who use Wompy know what is happening and urge them to pass this information on to other mountain bikers. If you hear anyone bragging about building a new trail at Wompatuck, (or for that matter anywhere else), take them to task. Illegal trails seriously undermine NEMBA's efforts of providing legitimate assistance to the park and could jeopardize all mountain bikers access to the trails here.

Thank you for your assistance.
Bill Boles, New England Mountain Bike Association

MilesDirections

0.0 START the ride at the last fire gate on the right. Follow paved fire road PR1 to a "T" intersection. Unfortunately the trails in Wompatuck are not named on the park map or in the woods so attention to landmarks and an accurate odometer are necessary on this ride. The trails are named here to match the map included with this ride.

0.5 At the "T" intersection, take a right onto PR2, another paved fire road.

1.2 Take a right down a smaller paved fire road (PR 3).

1.5 The fire road ends and faces a doubletrack dirt path. On the left is a paved parking area. Go straight ahead onto dirt path DT1.

1.7 Follow DT1 around to the right and uphill.

2.4 Take a right into the woods onto ST1, a pine needle-strewn singletrack. This trail winds through the woods, but there are no intersecting trails.

2.8 Take a sharp left on paved fire road PR4. This road is not as wide as the original fire road that began at the fire gate.

2.9 Take a soft left (about 10:30 on an imaginary clock) onto DT2 once you enter a paved clearing. This doubletrack brings you to a challenging climb.

3.4 Take a right at the "Y" in the trail, continuing on DT2. This trail goes uphill on a loose, gravel surface. This is Prospect Hill.

4.0 Nearly at the top of the hill, take a left on ST2, which starts between two large trees. This trail has numerous switchbacks and goes back to the bottom of the hill.

4.4 Take a right at the bottom onto DT3.

4.6 At four small pine trees and a tree with a white dot, take a right onto ST3. This trail winds up the back side of the hill through trees and over rocks.

5.1 After a climb over many obstacles, rooted sections, and hairy turns, the trail comes to a "T" intersection. Take a left onto ST4 over a stone wall.

5.2 The trail splits again, continue straight until ST4 turns comes a "Y" at the bottom of a short grade.

5.4 Take a right at the "Y" and follow ST5, a packed dirt singletrack trail.

5.6 At the gravel clearing, take a sharp right on gravel and dirt path DT4.

5.65 At the paved clearing, take a left into the woods onto ST6. While looking straight as you entered the clearing, the path into the woods starts at 9:30.

5.7 Take a left on paved fire road PR2.

6.4 Take a left onto flat singletrack ST7, which leads away from the paved fire road.

6.5 Follow ST7 as it takes a sharp right.

6.6 Bear right and continue on the singletrack. Other small paths seem to flow off the trail, but they dead-end later in the woods.

6.7 Turn right again on the trail and climb up the hill.

7.2 Head right and downhill into "THE ROCK GARDEN" then continue straight on the trail.

7.6 At the chain-link fence, the trail bears to the right.

7.8 Take a left onto ST8 into an often overgrown section of the woods.

8.0 Crest a small hill and see a wooden bridge below you. Ride down to the bridge and over it. Continue up the hill on the other side to the edge of a large field.

8.1 Ride straight across the field to the parking lot.

8.3 Take a right onto PR3.

8.6 Take a left onto PR2.

9.1 Take a left onto PR1.

9.6 Finish the ride by riding to the right of the fire gate and back to the car.

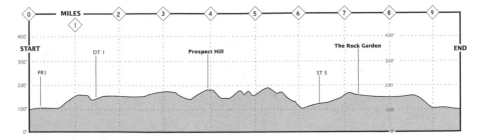

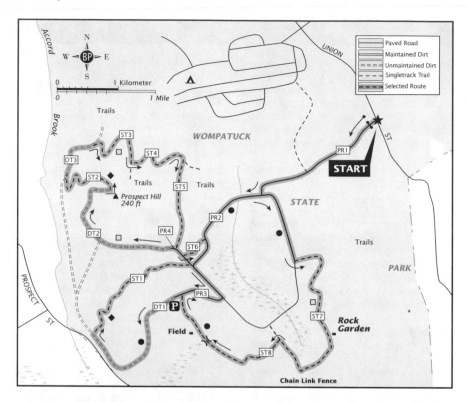

Borderland State Park

17

Ride Specs

Start: From the visitor center facing the parking lot
Length: 3.9-mile loop
Approximate Riding Time: 1–1½ hours
Difficulty Rating: Difficult because of the plentiful technical sections and dangerous descents
Terrain: Both technical singletrack and smooth, dirt and gravel doubletrack. Rocks are the most prevalent feature of the trail although roots do make an appearance from time to time.
Elevation Gain: 112 feet
Nearest Town: Sharon, MA
Other Trail Users: Hikers and equestrians

Getting There

From Boston: Take I-93 South to MA 24 South (Exit 4). Follow MA 24 south to MA 106 (Exit 16B). Take MA 106 west for nearly five miles to Poquanticut Road on the right. Follow Poquanticut for just over a mile, and take a left onto Massapoag Avenue. Borderland State Park is on the right, two miles away. Park near the visitor center. **DeLorme: Massachusetts Atlas & Gazetteer.** Page 53, L-16

Borderland was introduced to me by a friend who called the riding "hellish." We had both just begun our riding careers and my friend tried to cruise through Borderland on a fully rigid bike. Needless to say he was less than thrilled, and said he had no interest in ever visiting the park again. Instead of being deterred, I was intrigued.

Luckily I kept an open mind about Borderland. After my first visit, I was enthralled by the challenge and the varied terrain. With the exception of in Lynn Woods, I had never seen so much slickrock; and only in Dogtown Common in Gloucester had I seen rocks like these. In dry weather the park is a treat for the skilled rider. In wet weather, it can be frightening.

The trail begins easily enough with a few small rocks in the trail and an equal number roots. The trails are marked fairly well, so finding the way is easy—although some new trails now branched off the established ones. To ensure that you are on the right path, stay on the trail that looks more traveled. The new paths are thin and sometimes dead-end at back yards and paved roads.

As you get deeper into Borderland, the trail begins to steepen and the rocks abruptly appear. The singletrack becomes a mass of granite boulders averaging the size of soccer balls. Other rocks, both larger and smaller, are present as well and so line choice is crucial from this point forward.

Most of the climbs here are short and steep, which demands that riders be prepared to shift at a moment's notice. The descents also come up quickly and the bouncing terrain makes chains jump off chainrings regularly. Borderland demands that you remain aware of the trail ahead and plan for upcoming obstacles.

It should be noted that on one section of West Side Trail there are man-made wooden bridges spanning a perpetually muddy area. Some of the boards in these bridges are loose and most have gaps between them wide enough to swallow a tire. Take care going through this area. If it's really wet, walk your bike across the bridges to avoid creating deep ruts in the mud.

So lube up your shock and put on extra padded shorts. The terrain here can jar your teeth loose at each turn. If you are less adept at riding over and through numerous large rocks in the trail, you might consider bringing comfortable shoes for the hiking you'll have to do. This ride beats you up but it's very rewarding if you can conquer the obstacles in the way. The overall experience can be heavenly if you have the skills to ride the terrain. It's challenging and sometimes scary, but Borderland State Park is one of my favorite rides. Now I've just got to convince my friend.

Ride Information

🐾 Trail Contacts:
Borderland State Park, North Easton, MA (508) 238-6566 • NEMBA, Action, MA 1-800-57-NEMBA or www.nemba.org

🕐 Schedule:
The park is open year-round sunrise to sunset. Entering the park after dark is prohibited. Mountain bikes are not allowed on the Pond Edge, Swamp, and Quiet Woods Trails.

❓ Local Information:
Metro South Chamber of Commerce, Brockton, MA (508) 586-0500

💡 Local Events/Attractions:
Ames Mansion at Borderland State Park, North Easton, MA (508) 238-6566

• Kendall Whaling Museum, Sharon, MA (781) 784-5642 • Moose Hill Wildlife Sanctuary, Sharon, MA (781) 784-5691

🚲 Local Bike Shops:
Landry's Bicycles, South Easton, MA (508) 230-8882 • Silver City Bicycles, Raynham, MA (508) 828-9722 • Travis Cycle, Brockton, MA (508) 586-6394

Ⓝ Maps:
USGS maps: Brockton, MA • Trail maps are available at the visitor center.

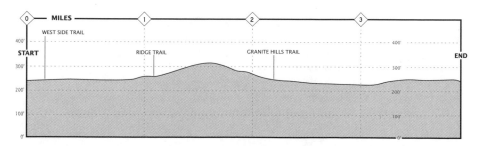

MilesDirections

0.0 START at the visitor center, facing the parking lot. Take a right onto West Side Trail, a singletrack path that climbs uphill gradually.

0.3 At the "Y" intersection, go left onto French Trail. Stay on this singletrack until it intersects with Northwest Trail.

0.7 Take a left on Northwest Trail and follow past Split Rock Trail to Ridge Trail on the right.

1.1 Take a right onto Ridge Trail, a singletrack that is interspersed with numerous sections of slickrock.

1.6 Follow Ridge Trail to the right at the top of the hill. The trail here is less rocky but has some hidden obstacles in the grass.

2.0 Veer right as Ridge Trail and Friends Trail become one for a short section.

2.1 Take a right on Friends Trail as it separates from Ridge Trail.

2.2 Take a right on Granite Hills Trail Upper Loop.

2.6 Continue straight downhill toward the gravel and dirt fire road, FR1.

2.7 Here there is a large section of slickrock. Remain to the left on Granite Hills Trail. Do not ride up on this rock.

2.8 Take a right at the fire road (FR1) and enter the singletrack again at West Side Trail.

3.3 Go right on West Side Trail into the woods. Follow this trail back around toward the visitor center.

3.9 Complete the ride at the visitor center.

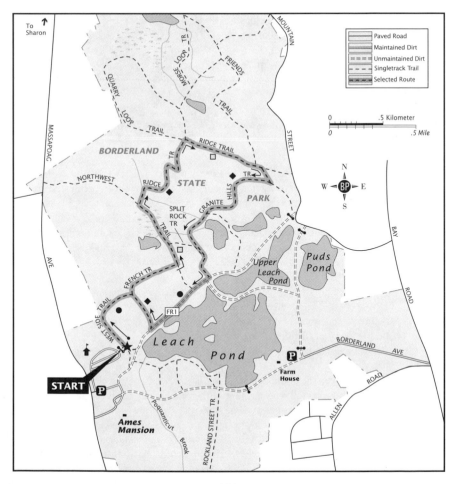

18 Freetown State Forest

Ride Specs

Start: From the main parking area off Slab Bridge Road in Assonet
Length: 6.9-mile circuit
Approximate Riding Time: 1½–2 hours
Difficulty Rating: Moderate to difficult. The ride incorporates a portion of the motorcycle trail and can present obstacles like large rocks, deep ruts, and loose sand. Finding a smooth line can be challenging in some areas, but other parts of the ride are smooth, big-ring cruisers.
Terrain: Primarily wooded singletrack. Surface has more rocks than roots, making proper line selection and tire pressure important. Fairly dry because of sandy soil, but in some areas there can be mud and standing water.
Elevation Gain: 417 feet
Nearest Town: Assonet, MA
Other Trail Users: Hikers, day-campers, walkers, equestrians, and motorcyclists

Getting There

From Boston: Take I-93 South to MA 24 (Exit 4). Follow MA 24 south to Exit 10. Bear left onto South Main Street and follow signs for Freetown State Forest. Take a left on MA 79 and then take a right onto Slab Bridge Road. The forest entrance is on the left and the parking area, as well as the wading pool and restroom facilities, is to the left of the main drive.
DeLorme: Massachusetts Atlas & Gazetteer: Page 57, N-23

Freetown State Forest is nearly as far south as Cape Cod and is geographically below Providence, Rhode Island. This allows for a peculiar mix of land characteristics. For example, the sandy base found on the Cape is present in some areas, but so are the mix of rocks and roots found at F. Gilbert Hills, Wompatuck State Park, and Purgatory Chasm. The rolling packed dirt surface is similar to that of trails at Callahan State Park, and the terrain is flatter than most of the rides in this book. All in all, it makes for some of the best riding in Southeastern Massachusetts

At some points during this ride the trail may be flat and smooth allowing a short, big-ring effort. This changes drastically into a treacherous field of rocks about half the size of a mountain bike wheel. The trails here challenge your ability to adapt and to navigate many different surfaces. But because the surfaces change so quickly, the amount of time spent on terrain you hate is limited, making the ride enjoyable overall.

At the beginning of the ride you'll see large square holes in the ground alongside the trail. These are full of water most of the year and are used for forest fire suppression. Created by state engineers, these stonewalled pits are essential because the forest is fairly vast and main roads with hydrants are not easily accessible. Another problem is that the sandy base in many areas allows water to run off quickly and leave dry sections of forest susceptible to fire. The forest personnel have their hands full watching the nearly 5,700 acres of land. With that amount of trees and land, getting a fire under

control is critical. Adding to the worry, many houses have been built around the forest's edge and residential streets lead to the Indian Reservation section of Freetown.

The primary dangers on this ride are of the human variety. The trails throughout the park have been carved by years of motorcycle use and the quick, winding trail creates many blind corners and sharp turns. If you're not paying attention you can easily come face to face with a speeding motorcycle. Another danger is hunters. The park is one of the most widely used areas in Southeastern Massachusetts and is open for hunting nearly all fall and winter. The safest fall and winter time to ride is on Sundays when hunting is not allowed.

Though this ride takes place in the main forest to the east of High Street, there is additional riding available on the west edge of the forest. There you'll find the Wampanoag Indian Reservation. It has extensive motorcycle trails and more elevation changes than the main forest, but the drawback to riding in the reservation is its sandy base, which can make climbing frustrating and descending a challenge. If you're curios about the Wampanoag's culture, they hold tribal events in the reservation and some of these events are public.

Ride Information

🗨 Trail Contacts:
Freetown-Fall River State Forest, Assonet, MA (508) 644-5522 • **NEMBA**, Action, MA 1-800-57-NEMBA

🕐 Schedule:
Trails are open year-round. Cross-country skiing, snowmobiling, and sled dogging occurs during the winter; hunting in the fall from October 1 to February 28. No camping is allowed. Hunting is not allowed on Sundays.

❓ Local Information:
Fall River Area Chamber of Commerce, Fall River, MA (508) 676-8226 • **Fall River Historical Society,** Fall River, MA (508) 679-1071

♀ Local Events/Attractions:
Lizzie Borden House, Fall River, MA (508) 675-7333 • **Battleship Massachusetts,** Fall River, MA (508) 678-1100

🚲 Local Bike Shops:
Beauvais Bicycle Shop, Taunton, MA (508) 824-5588 • **Cesar's Cyclery,** New Bedford, MA (508) 998-8777 • **Village Peddler,** Fairhaven, MA (508) 997-2453 • **Yesteryear Cyclery,** New Bedford, MA (508) 993-2525

Ⓝ Maps:
USGS maps: Somerset, MA • Maps of the park are available at the map across from forest headquarters, (508) 644-5522.

MilesDirections

0.0 START at the map across from the forest headquarters by taking a left onto Payne Road, a dirt fire road.

0.4 Take a right onto Hathaway Road, another dirt fire road.

0.6 Take a left at the end of Hathaway onto a singletrack trail called Breakneck.

0.8 Remain on Breakneck as it crosses an unpaved road (UP1) and continues straight.

0.9 Breakneck re-crosses UP1 and joins an unmarked trail. Cross the road and follow this trail as it weaves back and forth through the forest. At times this singletrack will cross the motorcycle trail.

2.9 Cross Payne Road and hop onto the marked Motorcycle Trail.

3.3 Leave the Motorcycle Trail by turning right onto a short unnamed singletrack path that empties into a field.

3.9 Take a right down the edge of the field and join High Street, a paved road.

4.0 Take a right onto High Street.

4.1 Take a right onto Payne Road and climb up a wicked hill.

4.6 Take a right on Hathaway Road then take a left onto the Motorcycle Trail.

4.9 The trail comes to a 6-way intersection. Go left on Hathaway Extension.

5.2 Take a left from Hathaway back onto the Motorcycle Trail and follow across Makepeace Road all the way to Payne Road.

6.0 Take a right on Payne Road and head back to the forest headquarters.

6.9 Finish the ride at the map across from Headquarters.

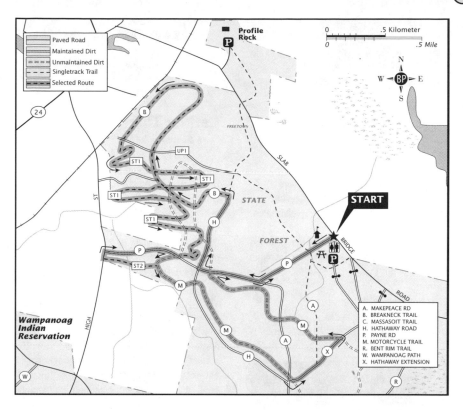

Legend
- Paved Road
- Maintained Dirt
- Unmaintained Dirt
- Singletrack Trail
- Selected Route

Profile Rock

0 .5 Kilometer
0 .5 Mile

N
W ← BP → E
S

24

B

UP1

ST1

ST1

ST1

B

STATE

H

FREETOWN

SLAB

START

P

ST2

P

M

FOREST

P

BRIDGE

M

A

A

M

ROAD

X

H

A. MAKEPEACE RD
B. BREAKNECK TRAIL
C. MASSASOIT TRAIL
H. HATHAWAY ROAD
P. PAYNE RD
M. MOTORCYCLE TRAIL
R. BENT RIM TRAIL
W. WAMPANOAG PATH
X. HATHAWAY EXTENSION

Wampanoag Indian Reservation

W

HIGH ST

R

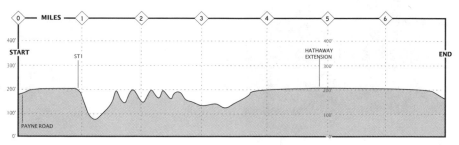

MILES 0 1 2 3 4 5 6

400'
START
ST1
HATHAWAY
EXTENSION
END
300'
200'
100'
PAYNE ROAD
0'

19

Ames Nowell State Park

Ride Specs

Start: From the parking area next to the restrooms
Length: 5.5-mile loop
Approximate Riding Time: 1–1½ hours
Difficulty Rating: Easy to moderate because of the roots on the east side of Cleveland Pond
Terrain: Smooth singletrack interspersed with some rocks and roots. Most of the technical riding takes place over sections that have multiple roots, but there are only a few of these sections.
Elevation Gain: 171 feet
Nearest Town: Abington, MA
Other Trail Users: Hikers and equestrians

Getting There

From Boston: Take MA 3 south to MA 18 (Exit 16). Travel south on MA 18 to Abington and MA 123. Take a right onto MA 123, heading toward Brockton. Take a right after about a mile onto Groveland Street and then in a moment turn right onto Linwood Street. A booth and a pair of stone gates mark the park entrance. Drive past these into the main parking area by the restrooms. *DeLorme: Massachusetts Atlas & Gazetteer.* Page 53, I-27

Via the Ⓣ: Take the MBTA Middleborough Line from South Station to Abington Station. Now on your bike, proceed west on MA 123. After crossing the intersection with MA 18, take a right onto Rockland Street and travel one mile and turn right on Linwood Street. A booth and a pair of stone gates mark the park entrance. Pedal past these into the main parking area by the restrooms. (Biking distance from Abington Station to start: 2.6 miles.)

Ames Nowell State Park is a relatively small recreation area, with just 607 acres. Most of the activities within the park center around Cleveland Pond. The large pond is situated in the eastern part of Ames Nowell and stretches nearly the length of the park from north to south. The pond also juts westward into the park for about a third of a mile. It's an ideal place for non-motorized boating, fishing, canoeing, swimming, and exploring.

While the existing trails around the pond are mainly hiking trails that dead end at the side of the pond, a continuous loop of the park can be made by linking power line tracks, a few hiking trails, doubletrack access roads, and bordering paved roads. This ride takes a full circle and provides a number of views of the pond from a variety of angles. About 60 percent of the ride has a view of the pond.

At the beginning of the ride, the two best scenic stops are the dam (at the southern-most part of the park) and the Boardwalk (on the southwest edge of the pond). Both allow riders to see herons, ducks, and hawks coasting above the water or floating in the high grass at the water's edge. These spots, as well as others, are great for photos of the water and foliage in the early fall, and they allow for super black and white shots in early winter when snow blankets the trails but the pond hasn't yet frozen.

Riding the trails isn't the only way to get a great look at the pond. Hiking along the water's edge or picnicking at the dozen or so wooden tables offers nice scenery as well. The picnic area and ball field are also convenient to both the restrooms and the parking area, so carrying a lunch or spending time here with children is not difficult.

As with all of the staffed state parks and forests in Massachusetts, Ames Nowell has helpful and knowledgeable employees. Most are able to identify the wildlife and plants within the park and all are willing to spend time with visitors to help make visits both enjoyable and educational. One Ames Nowell employee, during one of my visits, even helped put to rest the fears of a woman who felt she had captured a Killer Bee. She was flipping out thinking a Killer Bee had made its way from Mexico all the way up to a park in Massachusetts. The ranger was able to convince her that Killer Bees have only recently made it into Texas and Florida and still have a ways to go to get this far north.

According to park personnel, there aren't any dangerous animals within the park boundaries. And the only creatures allowed to be taken from Ames Nowell are the fish in Cleveland Pond, which include an array of bass, white crappy, brown bullhead (also called catfish), and perch. The state requires that you have a license if you plan to fish in the pond. These can be purchased in a variety of locations, call the state fisheries and wildlife office to find a location near you. So, whether you plan to walk, bike, hike, or fish, Ames Nowell is very accommodating and a great place to spend a relaxing day.

Ride Information

Trail Contacts:
Ames Nowell State Park, Abington, MA (781) 857-1336 • NEMBA, Action, MA 1-800-57-NEMBA or www.nemba.org

Schedule:
The park is open year-round but hours vary depending on the season. Typically the summer hours are from 8 a.m. to 8 p.m. Fall, winter, and spring hours are shortened typically to 8 a.m. to 4 p.m. Call for exact times. The Park is closed on Thanksgiving and Christmas.

Local Information:
Metro South Chamber of Commerce, Brockton, MA (508) 586-0500 • Division of Fisheries and Wildlife, Boston, MA (617) 727-3151, ext. 340

Local Events/Attractions:
Fuller Museum of Art, Brockton, MA (508) 588-6000

Local Bike Shops:
Landry's Bicycles, South Easton, MA (508) 230-8882 • Silver City Bicycles, Raynham, MA (508) 828-9722 • Travis Cycle, Brockton, MA (508) 586-6394

Maps:
USGS maps: Whitman, MA • Trail maps are available at the entrance to the park just behind the Contact Station.

MilesDirections

0.0 START in the main parking area, facing the restrooms. Ride to the left into the clearing between two stands of trees. This path, Cutthrough 1 comes out on a paved bike and walking path that circles around the ball field.

0.1 Take a right around the ball field and follow the paved path a short distance until it comes to a "T."

0.2 Take a right at the "T" intersection and ride onto gravel and dirt doubletrack (Water Access 1) that passes below the Dam.

0.3 Stay left as Water Access 1 splits.

0.6 Take a hairpin right turn off of Water Access 1 onto a 10-foot unnamed section and then take an immediate left onto the wooden boardwalk. Follow this trail straight until it ends and you face the water.

1.0 At the pond's edge, turn around and head back to the boardwalk.

1.4 After crossing the boardwalk, take a right and follow Water Access 1 straight to the power lines.

1.45 Take a right on the path that is parallel to the power lines.

1.5 After riding up on the large slickrock, take a right on the doubletrack dirt access road (Access 2). Follow it straight to the end at North Quincy Street.

2.1 Take a right onto the paved North Quincy Street.

2.5 Take a right onto paved Chestnut Street.

3.9 Take a right onto paved Hancock Street.

4.3 Take a right onto a singletrack trail (Cutthrough 2) that is marked by a telephone pole on the left and a dilapidated fence on the right. This trail is park property and goes between two yards. The trail here becomes rocky and rooty and is a little harder than Water Access 1. The grade is mostly flat.

4.5 Take a right at the "T" intersection onto Horse Trail, and then take an almost immediate hairpin left turn onto Water's Edge, a singletrack trail that goes along the water's edge. This trail goes all the way back to the picnic area and ball field and has multiple rooty sections and winding singletrack. It also provides prime photo opportunities of the pond.

5.2 At the picnic area, take a left onto the paved path, keeping the ball field on the right.

5.3 The path will come to the main park entrance. Take a left onto the paved access road toward the parking area.

5.5 End the ride at the parking area in front of the restrooms.

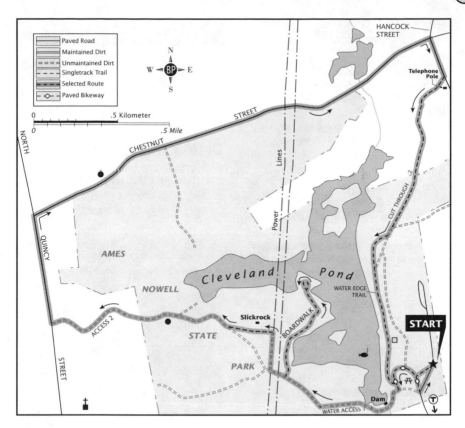

Paved Road
Maintained Dirt
Unmaintained Dirt
Singletrack Trail
Selected Route
Paved Bikeway

N
W — BP — E
S

0   .5 Kilometer
0   .5 Mile

HANCOCK STREET

Telephone Pole

STREET

CHESTNUT

NORTH

Lines

CUT THROUGH

QUINCY

AMES

NOWELL

Cleveland   Pond

WATER EDGE TRAIL

Slickrock

BOARDWALK

START

STATE

ACCESS 2

STREET

PARK

Dam

WATER ACCESS

T

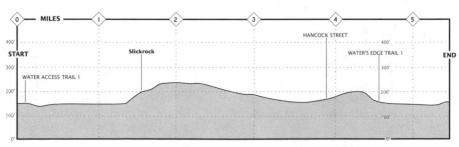

Myles Standish State Forest

Ride Specs

Start: From the parking lot adjacent to the Forest Headquarters in the southern part of the park

Length: 11-mile loop

Approximate Riding Time: 1½–2 hours

Difficulty Rating: Easy to moderate because of the amount of paved bike paths. Singletrack and sandy power lines make riding more difficult, but they can be avoided by reversing your path at mile 3.9 and returning to the parking lot—reducing the total distance to about eight miles.

Terrain: This ride has a few types terrain: 30% paved bike paths, 20% paved roads; and 50 % sandy double and singletrack. Most areas are easy, undulating hills, but some of the singletrack can be difficult to climb because of its sandy composition.

Elevation Gain: *339 feet*

Nearest Town: Plymouth, MA

Other Trail Users: Hikers, equestrians, motorcyclists, and hunters (in season)

Getting There

From Boston: Take I-93 South to MA 3 South (Exit 7). Take MA 3 to Long Pond Road (Exit 5) and head west. After about 3.5 miles, take a right on Alden Road at the sign for Myles Standish Sate Forest. Follow park signs for the Forest Headquarters. Once at the Forest Headquarters, park in either lot. *DeLorme: Massachusetts Atlas & Gazetteer.* Page 58, J-14

Myles Standish State Forest is over 16,000 acres in size and has numerous ponds, paths, and trails to explore. It's also one of only a couple places in this guide that offers the opportunity for establishing a camping base for your mountain bike rides. It can be economically attractive to stow your gear at a campsite while you take short trips to historic downtown Plymouth. By bike it's a bit of a trek, but it's only about 15 minutes by car. The cost of a campsite is considerably less than that of a hotel, and you'll be roughing it in the same general area as the men and women who sailed here from England.

If you decide Plymouth can wait, explore the trails through the park, including the paved bike path (a good portion of this ride) or explore the many horse / hiking / biking trails that wind through the dense forest. The forest is a prime area for ticks, so be sure to wear bug repellent or be extra vigilant when checking after a ride through the woods.

There are two distinct parts to this ride: the smooth, sedate part; and the more challenging, lung-busting, leg-pumping part. The easier section is made up of smooth, almost pristine asphalt bike paths. These paths wind through the forest occasionally crossing a bridle path or road. The more difficult section is sandy, rocky, and rutted. As it was for the Pilgrims who landed in Plymouth in 1620, your path will be both smooth and rocky.

After your ride, you might have time for a trip to Plymouth. If you decide to explore the nation's roots, plan to bring your imagination, some cash, and a lot of energy. Walking from site to site, and standing in line, can wear on the legs almost as much as hammering singletrack.

Once in Plymouth Center find Plymouth Rock and make this your reference point. Most of the brochures historic sites use this significant boulder as a part of their directions. The Rock has deteriorated over time and is now caged from both the sea and vandals in a large granite memorial. There is a 1620 carved into the Rock, and it's given credit for being the rock on which the Pilgrims first set foot in America.

Getting to the New World wasn't an easy task. It was a journey that was bumpy even before it began. American history seldom mentions the Mayflower's sister ship, the Speedwell. It left port at the same time as the Mayflower, on August 15, but due to leaks was forced back to shore twice. Eventually it was decided that the passengers would all pile onto the Mayflower.

On September 16 the Mayflower finally set sail from Plymouth, England, with 102 passengers. The trip took just over two months, and during that time two people died and two were born. Upon reaching America the ship dropped anchor just off Provincetown on the tip of Cape Cod. The reason for the stop was to set up some preliminary governing body before reaching land. Forty-one men aboard the ship signed the Mayflower Compact, and John Carver was elected the Pilgrim's first governor.

Though John Carver may be best known as the first leader of the new colony, it was William Bradford who would eventually do more for the Pilgrims. In fact Bradford was the person who coined the term "Pilgrim" to describe his group of Leiden Separatists who originally left Holland for Southampton, England, on the Speedwell. Bradford and his group joined the English separatists on the Mayflower. When Carver died in office after less than a year, Bradford was elected to succeed him. He subsequently served 30 years as governor.

One of Bradford's assistants was none other than Myles Standish, an English-born professional soldier who came to America as an advisor to the Pilgrims. Originally Standish worked on colonial defense and relations with the Native Americans, but he soon become more political and represented Plymouth Colony in England. Eventually Standish branched out and founded another local community, Duxbury, in 1632. The state forest that bears his name is situated in both Plymouth and Carver while Duxbury lies a few towns to the north.

These days when you look left while standing facing Plymouth Rock you will see a replica of the Mayflower. Built from a model created in 1926, the Mayflower was sailed to Plymouth, Massachusetts, from Plymouth, England, in 1957. You can tour the ship and see what sort of boat the Pilgrims spent so much time aboard.

Ride Information

📞 Trail Contacts:
Myles Standish State Forest, Plymouth, MA (508) 866-2526 • **NEMBA**, Acton, MA 1-800-57-NEMBA or *www.nemba.org*

🕐 Schedule:
The park is open year-round, but the recreational trails are closed Saturdays and holidays from mid October through January 2, as well as the entire week of deer hunting season when hunters are allowed to use shotguns.

❓ Local Information:
Plymouth County Development Council, Plymouth, MA 1-800-USA-1620

💡 Local Events/Attractions:
Colonial Lantern Tours, Plymouth, MA (508) 747-4161 – *evenings from April to November, $8 for adults* • **Plimoth**

Plantation, Plymouth, MA (508) 746-1622 – *Plimoth Plantation runs both the 1627 Pilgrim Village and the Mayflower II in Plymouth Harbor. Both are open from March through November from 9:00 a.m. to 5:00 p.m. every day of the week. Admission to the village is $16 for adults and $9 for kids 12 and younger. For the Mayflower II, adults are $6.50 and kids are $4. A special pass is available for both attractions at a savings of $3.*

🚲 Local Bike Shops:
Serious Cycles, Plymouth, MA (508) 746-2756

🗺 Maps:
USGS maps: Plymouth, MA; Wareham, MA • **Myles Standish State Forest map** – available for free at Forest Headquarters

MilesDirections

0.0 START by facing the "Welcome" sign before the Forest Headquarters. Go left through the parking lot to fire gate 87. Ride up the hill on the paved Bike Path. The Bike Path undulates and weaves back and forth through the forest. Steep grades are marked by painted signs on the ground so inexperienced riders will be able to prepare for short downhills or harsh uphills. This trail winds for about four miles and the dirt portion of this ride begins at the power lines.

4.0 The Bike Path ends at Bare Hill Road. Take a right on Bare Hill Road for a moment.

4.1 Take a right underneath the power lines on the Sandy Access Road.

4.6 Take a left on Hog Rock Road, an unpaved road that's also used as a bridle trail.

4.7 Continue straight on Hog Rock Road at the 4-way intersection with Kamesit Road. The trail begins to thin here and can be overgrown.

Medium size rocks sometimes are present in rain ruts. Another feature of this trail is the undulating smooth dirt surface.

5.6 At the "Y" intersection, go right on ST1.

6.9 The trail goes under the power lines and continues on the other side.

7.1 At the "T" intersection go left onto ST2.

7.2 At the "Y" intersection, go right on Wayont Road, an unpaved road.

7.8 Take a left onto the wide, unpaved access road, Federal Pond Road.

8.1 Take a right on the paved Lower College Pond Road.

9.8 At the stop sign continue straight.

9.9 At the "Y" intersection with Halfway Pond Road, stay on Lower College Pond Road.

10.2 Take a left back onto the Bike Path and follow it to Forest Headquarters.

11.0 Emerge from fire gate 87 at the parking lot next to Headquarters.

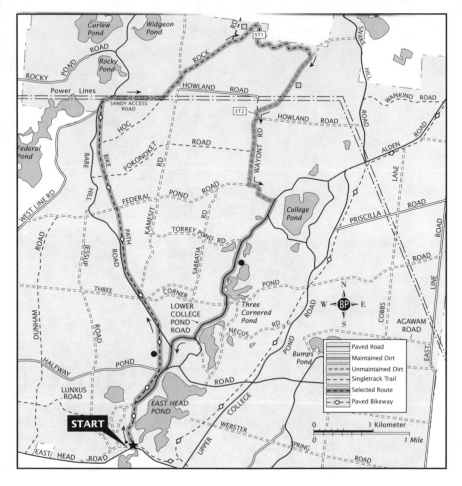

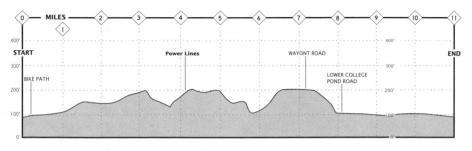

MetroWest

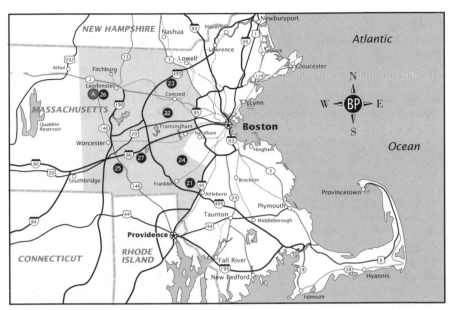

I n terms of sheer elevation, MetroWest—that region west of Route 128 and roughly bound by Interstate 495—holds top honors in this guide, followed closely by the
region North of Boston. Once you exit the Boston Basin this becomes evident as
you enter the expanse of rolling hills that rise between Boston and the Connecticut
River Valley. But the elevation gain is modest at best. What is striking, rather, is the
quick shift from urban sprawl to countryside. City lights and pavement abruptly give
way to open greenspace, multiple lakes, and freshwater marshes.

The region's rural landscape can be attributed to a number of factors. Its function
as a retreat for the wealthy families of Boston no doubt had a positive affect, but its
preservation is mostly due the economy that kept it alive, agriculture. Since World
War II, many of the farms have succumbed to the encroachment of the city.
Surprisingly though, and thanks to various park preserves, much of the character of the
region has been maintained.

This region makes for great riding and nature watching because once in the woods
you won't hear cars or civilization. Except for the occasional gunshot. Hunting becomes
more prevalent throughout the state as you head west, deer hunting in particular.
Remember the blue laws and ride only on Sundays during the fall and winter.

21

F. Gilbert Hills State Forest

Ride Specs

Start: From the Forest Headquarters on Mill Street
Length: 10.6-mile loop
Approximate Riding Time: 2–3 hours
Difficulty Rating: Moderate to difficult. Riding challenges range from steep climbs on loose, rocky, and sandy slopes to severely pitched downhills with multiple roots and off-camber turns.
Terrain: A healthy amount of singletrack with some doubletrack fire roads at the beginning and end of the ride. Roots and rocks are plentiful. About 20% level with the remainder either made up of climbs or descents. Primarily dry but there are two or three areas that are muddy year-round.
Elevation Gain: 483 feet
Nearest Town: Foxborough, MA
Other Trail Users: Hikers, equestrians, motorcyclists, joggers, and walkers

Getting There

From Boston: Take I-90 or I-93 to I-95 South. Take I-95 South to MA 140 (Exit 7). Go west on MA 140 into Foxborough. Once in town, take a left onto South Street and follow it south out of Foxborough Center for 1.5, to Mill Street. Take a right and follow Mill Street for less than a mile to the Forest Headquarters. When the fire gates are open, park next to the Headquarters; otherwise, park on the left-hand side of Mill Street in the dirt parking area. *DeLorme: Massachusetts Atlas & Gazetteer.* Page 52, L-9

For the mountain bike enthusiast there are few trail systems in Massachusetts better than the one inside F. Gilbert Hills State Forest. Cyclists in the region refer to the forest by the name of the town in which it's located—Foxborough. So, if someone says they rode "Foxborough," you now understand where they mean. The park honors Gilbert Hills, a forester for the Department of Environmental Management (DEM) from 1925 to 1969 who produced a series of maps on various state-owned properties, many of which are still in use today.

The terrain in F. Gilbert Hills covers all difficulty levels. The park's 1,027 acres, with 23 miles of multiple-use trails, allow cyclists to venture through the woods without running into too many other users. And yet trail use has increased to the point that the DEM unofficially asks that cyclists try to use other local parks, such as Wrentham State Forest, Franklin State Forest, Douglas State Forest, and Upton State Forest. But the riding at Foxborough is far too good and far too representative of a Massachusetts mountain biking experience to ignore. To limit the impact on the area and to make the ride more enjoyable for yourself as well as others, try to schedule your visit to Foxborough on a weekday when fewer cyclists use the park.

As is typical of Massachusetts's wilderness areas, Foxborough has been shaped by glacial activity. The large boulders, loose sandy soil, and sharp changes in elevations

are a result of this activity. Because of this, the riding is more challenging. The soil mixture that remains is technically called glacial till. A great way to understand how it came to be is to think of a giant using boulders the size of mountains as sandpaper. The land was rubbed with these giant pieces of earth until the result was a vast array of soil ranging from sand to slickrock.

These characteristics allow the soil to drain fairly well, which makes riding possible all year long. Helping matters further, come winter, the tree cover helps keep snow from accumulating so heavily on the singletrack. In the winter the trails are used frequently by cross-country skiers, and of course, hunting is only allowed during the fall. So always keep an eye open for others.

In one area of the park the trail climbs over large, flat boulders that are rubber-grabbing playgrounds during dry conditions and scary, slippery, and icy expanses after the slightest rain. Other sections offer tight, tree- and rock-laden switchbacks and descents that have influenced the designs of regional frame builders. Lloyd Graves, a designer and co-owner of Independent Fabrication, Inc. (IF) of Somerville, Massachusetts, has been adapting frames to the unique New England terrain since 1995. IF has raised the bottom bracket, for instance, to help cyclists negotiate the tighter turns frequently found in this area. As the bracket is raised the ground clearance is raised, but bike handling can be adversely affected. For steep drop-offs and sharp turns, a high bottom bracket is desired. For fast fire roads, a lower bottom bracket helps increase stability by lowering the bike's center of gravity. This change has proven extremely useful to mountain bikers in the Pacific Northwest as well.

Ride Information

🌸 Trail Contacts:
F. Gilbert Hills State Forest, Foxborough, MA (508) 543-5850 • **NEMBA**, Acton, MA 1-800-57-NEMBA or *www.nemba.org*

🕐 Schedule:
Trail is open year-round. Cross-country skiing during the winter; hunting in the fall.

❓ Local Information:
Foxborough, Mansfield & Norton Chamber of Commerce, Foxborough, MA (508) 543-3442 • **Foxborough Recreation Department,** Foxborough, MA (508) 543-7255 • Tune your radio to **AM 1030 (WBZ)** for weather every 10 minutes.

🎯 Local Events/Attractions:
New England Patriots Tickets: 1-800-543-1776 • **Foxboro Stadium Events Line:** (508) 543-3900

🚲 Local Bike Shops:
Independent Fabrication (Frame manufacturer), Somerville, MA (617) 666-3609 • **Bicycles Plus,** Franklin, MA (508) 520-1212 • **Franklin Bicycle,** Franklin, MA (508) 520-BIKE • **Sirois Bicycle Shop,** North Attleboro, MA (508) 695-6303

🅝 Maps:
USGS maps: Franklin, MA • Maps of the park are available at the ranger station.

IF has also shortened the chainstays. Bikes made for riding tight singletrack have chainstays about 16 inches long. This feature can make climbing easier, however the ride can become harsher because the bike absorbs more punishment over a smaller area. There is a point of diminishing returns where the shifting is affected if the chainstay is too short. Shimano has issued guidelines that say chainstays much shorter than the ones used by IF could cause extra chain and drivetrain wear on Shimano components.

As far as bike design and materials are concerned, Foxborough is accommodating to all styles and makes of bikes—although full suspension bikes are becoming more and more prevalent as their prices drop. The large number of rocky and rooty sections, as well as the loose gravel and large boulders, make full suspension bikes more suitable to the terrain than a hardtail or a fully rigid bike. Ultimately, the skill and technique of a rider are going to determine how effectively his or her bike negotiates the trail.

Just north of the forest on U.S. Route 1 is Foxboro Stadium, home to the New England Patriots (NFL) and the New England Revolution (Soccer). The stadium has hosted concerts by such big-name acts as The Police, The Rolling Stones, U2, and The Grateful Dead. Originally, the stadium was called Schaefer Stadium (after the beer of the same name). Three name changes later, it is now Foxboro Stadium.

To clear up any confusion, Foxborough, as well as quite a few other Massachusetts towns, can be spelled with either an "ough" or "oro." Whether you call the ride F. Gilbert Hills, Foxborough, or Foxboro, this trail system is a great location for testing your mountain biking stamina and skills. Just be sure to keep your ears open for motorcycles, and try to visit the park during less-traveled periods. No matter when it's ridden, F. Gilbert Hills State Forest is fantastic.

MilesDirections

0.0 START the ride with the fire building on the left and the ranger station on the right. A map of the forest is beside the fire gate to Wolf Meadow Road. Go uphill through this fire gate onto Wolf Meadow Road. The doubletrack climbs uphill and has a packed base of dirt with some loose sections.

0.15 Here is an intersection at a large boulder. Beginning here there are small triangular signs with a mountain bike printed on them. Take the doubletrack to the right (Tupelo Trail) and continue to follow the signs throughout your ride.

0.4 The Tupelo Trail turns left and is joined by Pine Hill Trail. The trail becomes thinner and has a few more roots and rocks than the earlier section.

0.7 Tupelo intersects with a paved road. Granite Street goes right and Lakeview goes left. Take a left on Lakeview.

0.8 Take a left into the woods back onto Tupelo Trail. Remain on this technical singletrack as it becomes more technical, rises uphill, and then drops precariously through washed-out,

sandy sections.

1.2 Remain on Tupelo Trail as it weaves right through the trees.

1.4 Follow the trail as it bears to the right at the bottom of a short downhill.

1.6 The singletrack comes to a "T" intersection. Take a left down the singletrack, continuing on the Tupelo Trail.

1.8 Tupelo Trail stops at a "T" intersection and becomes wide singletrack at a sign for Loop A and Loop B. Take a right here onto a trail simply called the Mountain Bike/Motorcycle Trail. This route is marked sporadically with green triangular signs with bikes on them.

1.9 At the "T" intersection in the Mountain Bike/Motorcycle Trail, take a right, still following part of the Motorcycle/Mountain Bike Trail.

2.0 Take another right onto Messenger Road, a wide doubletrack with a more packed dirt base.

2.1 The trail splits left and straight. Take a left uphill onto a short section of the Tupelo Trail. The trail is singletrack with a challenging loose, rocky base.

MilesDirections *continued*

2.3 Tupelo Trail again connects with the Mountain Bike/Motorcycle Trail and heads slightly downhill and winds around to the right.

2.35 Take a hard left on ST1, a ridge-like single-track, and follow the main trail. There are a few trails that shoot off ST1, but they just dead-end in the woods.

2.4 The singletrack splits at a "Y" intersection. Take a left, still on ST1, over a short wooden bridge. Either ride or carry the bike over the triangle of logs that front Pond Trail. This path is thin and level and traverses a ridge next to the unnamed pond.

2.6 At the other side of the pond there's another stack of logs and a "T" intersection with the Warner Trail. Take a left on the doubletrack Warner Trail.

2.65 At this "T" intersection, take a right uphill onto the Mountain Bike/Motorcycle Trail. The trail becomes more rooty and undulates as it winds through the woods.

3.1 At this "T" intersection, go left onto more undulating singletrack. This is still part of the Mountain Bike/Motorcycle Trail.

3.5 At the "Y" intersection, go left on ST2, a singletrack section of the forest that often has multiple large puddles in the middle of the trail.

3.9 Here is a four-way intersection with signs for Loop C to the right. Take a right uphill between the large rocks and onto Loop C. This is a fairly technical, albeit short, climb.

4.0 This "T" intersection offers smoother singletrack. Go right up the hill continuing on Loop C of the Mountain Bike/Motorcycle Trail.

4.3 Take a left up the steep hill just on the other side of the rock garden at the "T" intersection with High Rock Road, a sandy doubletrack fire road.

4.35 About two-thirds of the way up this hill, take a right into the trees on ST3, a short section of dirt singletrack.

4.4 Pop out onto DT1, a doubletrack road. Go straight across onto ST4 into the trees. Follow ST4 straight as it exhibits some areas of flat, smooth rock and many areas of rooty climbs and descents.

4.75 ST5 shoots off to the right. Remain on ST4 to the left.

4.8 Go straight across a paved road and rejoin the Mountain Bike/Motorcycle Trail on the other side.

4.9 There is a large tree here fronting a massive flat rock section. The roots at the base of the tree guard access to the flat rock. Go straight over the roots and keep pedaling to make it up onto the rock. This is an ideal resting spot as you're about halfway through the ride.

4.95 Head down the other side of the rock area and back into the woods on the Mountain Bike/Motorcycle Trail.

5.0 The Mountain Bike/Motorcycle Trail begins again and heads downhill fairly steeply.

5.1 At this "T" intersection, take a left uphill to a sandy fire road.

5.2 The fire road reaches an intersection that offers five options. Bear right, diagonally across the road and begin riding on the Tupelo Trail 2.

5.25 After a short downhill the Tupelo Trail 2 connects with the Mountain Bike/Motorcycle Trail, which comes in from the right. Continue straight on the Mountain Bike/Motorcycle Trail.

5.3 At this "Y" intersection, go left onto ST6, a tight, technical singletrack uphill.

5.9 At a 4-way intersection, remain on ST6, which turns right and then heads left. It is clearly the main trail here, but a section of the Mountain Bike/Motorcycle Trail leaves this trail at a right angle.

6.1 Here is the first of a series of large, wide, flat rocks that sprout up in the middle of the singletrack.

6.35 A large rock is on the right as the trail winds downhill. Take a right up onto the rock. Once on top, take a left down the center of it to join ST6 again.

6.4 Take a right onto ST6.

6.7 At this 4-way intersection, go straight.

7.1 Here is a rock garden made up of softball to bowling ball-sized rocks. Treacherous during wet conditions even though the terrain here is flat.

7.8 At this 4-way intersection, go right onto ST7

7.91 Take a left onto ST7 at the "Y" intersection at the top of a hill.

8.0 Remain to the right on ST7, this technical, turning downhill.

8.6 ST7 intersects with Megley Trail, a loose,

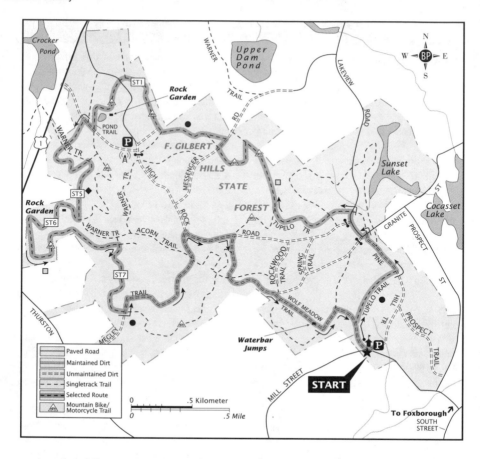

rocky and sandy fire road. Take a left on Megley.

9.2 Take a right on High Rock Road, another fire road.

9.4 At the "T" intersection, take a right on Wolf Meadow Road, a doubletrack fire road made up of more packed dirt and some loose rocks.

9.9 At this 3-way intersection, remain right on Wolf Meadow Road.

10.1 Encounter the first of five waterbar jumps in the middle of the road as Wolf Meadow Road heads downhill.

10.4 Stay to the right on Wolf Meadow Road as it heads downhill to the ranger station.

10.6 The ride ends back at the ranger station and fire gate.

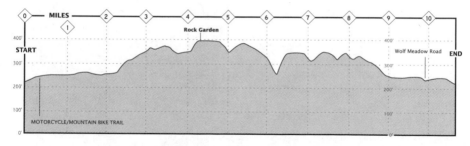

Callahan State Park

Ride Specs

County: Middlesex
Start: From the dirt parking lot off of Millwood Street in Framingham
Length: 6.5-mile circuit
Approximate Riding Time: 1–1½ hours
Difficulty Rating: Most of the park falls into the moderate rating, but the technical riding on the north side of Edmands Road can be brutal.
Terrain: Packed-dirt double and singletrack. Rocky and rooty climbs and descents. Smooth, thin dirt paths through open fields.
Elevation Gain: 352 feet
Nearest Town: Framingham, MA
Other Trail Users: Hikers, equestrians, and dog walkers

Getting There

From Boston: Take I-90 West to MA 9 East (Exit 12). Take MA 9 toward Framingham to Edgell Road. Go left on Edgell Road. Follow it to Belknap Road where you'll take a left. Follow Belknap Road for a short distance until you see Millwood Street. Take a right onto Millwood and follow it to the dirt parking area across from the golf course.
DeLorme: Massachusetts Atlas & Gazetteer: Page 39, K-28

Welcome to Dr. Jekyll and Mr. Hyde. Callahan State Park has two distinct personalities: a kind, subtle one and a nasty, cranky, ogre-like one. If you're riding extremely well, the ogre can be tamed, but if your skills are lacking, he'll make you pay. I suggest that if you arrive at Edmands Road (mile 2.2) and feel like you've had a tough workout, turn around and head left up the Pipeline Trail. This is the toughest climb in the southern part of the park, but it is not nearly as tough as the climb across the road.

At the beginning of this ride, an earthen dam winds left around the bottom of the park. On top of this dam is a doubletrack gravel and dirt path. This path serves as an access road that leads to a bunch of mild trails that wind through the southern part of the park. The trails have plenty of roots as well as a few rocks. They also offer some climbs—but they are intermediate grade for the most part. The only real difficult areas in this section are the climb up Juniper Trail and the perpetually muddy spots currently being worked on by NEMBA.

Once Juniper Trail ends and you shoot down Red Tail Trail, the transformation begins. After crossing Edmands Road there's a thin, smooth singletrack trail that runs next to a sheep corral. It seems mild enough until you reach the end. The trail bears slightly left and then roars up in front of you with rocks as big as the sheep in the pen and an off-camber surface that feeds riders into the woods to the right.

The best line to take up this hill is the high one. Ride straight up the left side of the hill and make a sharp turn to the right. Remain high on the trail and ride over the rocks that line the left edge. Fight the temptation to flow down to the right—the dirt is soft and the angle almost necessitates ratchet pedaling. The slope is so steep that if your left pedal gets lower than the bottom bracket, it will probably strike the ground and tip you into the trees to the right. The pedals, therefore, should be turned in short ratcheting motions, keeping the left crank up and the right crank down.

As you near the top of this steep section, the path becomes level from left to right but still climbs upward over multiple rocks and roots. The trees are still to the right and the drop has increased in height. Remain on this trail until it begins to head downhill and then take a quick breather. The climbing has just begun. After a short downhill section, the ride turns left and climbs even higher. This trail, which peaks at about 480 feet, subsequently drops down to a field where Mr. Hyde reverts back to the gentle doctor.

On the way back to the road, Mr. Hyde will peek his ugly head back out for one final look. But after dealing with his fury once before, the second time should be a piece of cake. If you'd rather spend the day with Hyde, travel into Marlborough and enter Callahan State Park at the North Entrance off of Broad Meadow Road. Whatever your choice, you're sure to find something you like about this changeable ride.

Ride Information

Trail Contacts:
Callahan State Park, Framingham, MA (508) 653-9641 • NEMBA, Acton, MA 1-800-57-NEMBA or www.nemba.org

Schedule:
The park is open year-round. Some parts of the park border private land so watch for signs.

Local Information:
MetroWest Chamber of Commerce, Framingham, MA (508) 879-5600

Local Events/Attractions:
Garden in the Woods, Framingham, MA (508) 877-6574 • Danforth Museum of Art, Framingham, MA (508) 620-0050

Local Bike Shops:
Landry's Bicycles, Framingham, MA (508) 875-5158 • Town & Country Bicycles, Medfield, MA (508) 359-8377 • Peter White Cycles, Acton, MA (978) 635-0969

Maps:
USGS maps: Framingham, MA • Trail maps are available at the South Entrance parking lot. Donations accepted.

MilesDirections

0.0 START at the back of the parking lot and go straight through the fire gate, past the map box and up the tiny hill toward the Earthen Dam. Take a left onto the Dam Trail and follow it as it curves toward the woods.

0.5 Take a right on The Drop, a worn singletrack that drops sharply off the edge of the doubletrack Dam Trail and then climbs just as sharply into the woods.

0.6 Once at the woods, take a right onto Coco Ridge Trail, singletrack that winds through the thick forest.

0.7 Take a right onto Moore Road, a singletrack trail that turns right and briefly becomes a thin path before turning into a doubletrack trail across a field by Eagle Pond.

0.9 At the edge of Moore Road, take a left toward the pond on the singletrack Pond Path and then remain on the path as it circles the pond's left edge.

1.0 Cross over a cement-filled water run-off, and climb up onto Eagle Trail.

1.2 Take a left uphill onto Fox Hunt Trail.

1.3 Take a right uphill onto Juniper Trail.

1.8 Take a left and then a quick right off of Juniper onto Red Tail Trail. This wider singletrack flows downhill over packed dirt and a few roots.

1.9 Take a right onto Pioneer Trail and follow it to the fire gate on the edge of Edmands Road.

2.2 Take a left onto Edmands Road, a paved residential street.

2.3 At the sheep pen take a right into the tall grass onto the smooth dirt singletrack of Backpacker Trail. Follow Backpacker straight to a brutal climb and then a more gradual technical uphill.

2.8 Take a left off of Backpacker Trail onto ST1, a loose, rocky singletrack trail that climbs up to the top of Gibbs Mountain.

2.9 At the top of Gibbs take a right down the hill onto ST2, a thin trail that winds through the trees.

3.1 At the bottom, take a left on the smooth ST3 trail, which climbs around the left edge of the field then plummets to a trail next to Beebe Pond.

3.4 Go left on Pine Tree Loop, the trail that circles the pond. Keep the pond on your right as you ride around its left bank.

3.8 The trail splits. Stay to the right and follow the main path.

4.3 The trail spits again. Take the trail to the left, ST4, and follow it as it winds downward to the edge of the field. Take a left up the edge of the field to the end of Backpacker Trail and follow Backpacker straight through the woods.

4.4 Follow Backpacker Trail through two consecutive right turns and then ride along the ridge that you rode on your way past the sheep corral.

4.9 Backpacker ends at Edmands Road. Go straight across onto Red Tail Trail.

5.6 Take a left on Fox Hunt Trail.

5.9 Take a right on Eagle Trail, which is just past a four-way intersection with Juniper Trail.

6.1 Keep Eagle Pond on the left and ride along its right edge.

6.2 Take a left on doubletrack fire road, Moore Road.

6.5 The ride ends as you cross through the fire gate at the dirt parking lot across from the golf course.

123

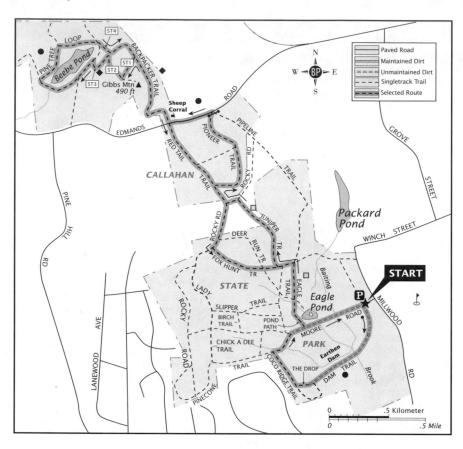

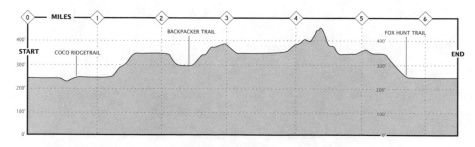

Great Brook Farm

23

Ride Specs

Start: From the main parking lot by the duck pond—just down the hill from the ice cream stand and the silo

Length: 17 miles of trail within 975 acres

Difficulty Rating: Easy to moderate because of the rolling, smooth dirt and extensive hiking traffic

Terrain: Rolling, smooth single and double-track. Some rooty and rocky uphills and medium grade downhills. A few fields and fire roads and some tougher sections of rocky, thin singletrack.

Nearest Town: Carlisle, MA

Other Trail Users: Hikers, equestrians, joggers, and cross-country skiers in the winter

Getting There

From Boston: Take I-90 to I-95 North. Take I-95 North to MA 225 West (Exit 31). Take MA 225 into the center of the town of Carlisle and go right onto Lowell Road. Follow this to North Road and take a right. Follow North Road to a duck pond and the main Great Brook Farm parking area. *DeLorme: Massachusetts Atlas & Gazetteer:* Page 28, L-5

Great Brook Farm gives us a glimpse into how life used to be in colonial Massachusetts. The farm was once the private home of the Farnham W. Smith family who operated a successful dairy on the premises until the 1970s. In 1974 the Massachusetts Division of Forests and Parks purchased the park to protect a piece of New England's history. There is even some evidence that the surrounding area was home to Native American communities and American colonists.

Great Brook Farm provides expanses of water and wilderness, perfect for enjoying a boat ride, a picnic, or a fun ride through the woods. While adaptable to almost any riding style, Great Brook is primarily a family park that caters to hikers, bikers, nature lovers, and almost anyone who wants to spend a day away from the hustle and bustle of the city. A little over an hour from downtown Boston, Great Brook has a working dairy; barnyard animals like goats, mules, and chickens; as well as a duck pond for scenic picnics or just relaxing. Children and adults can feed the animals with food from a pellet dispenser that's conveniently located next to the animal pen.

As you pull into the parking area you'll see the barn's silo, as well as the ice cream stand, up on the hill in the building behind the duck pond. The ice cream stand opens for business in late spring and stays open daily from 11 a.m. to park closing time around dusk. Another way to cool off is to take a canoe into Meadow Pond, about half a mile back up the North Road on your right. There's a small bridge for launching your boat as well as a tiny parking area.

With 975 acres of land and water in Great Brook State Park, there's plenty to do, from a variety of physical activities to educational programs sponsored by the park staff. During the summer, visitors can stroll about and see some of the local color: grazing cows, blue herons, horned owls, and beaver to name a few. If you don't want to miss anything, enlist in a guided tour of the barn and the park by calling the Park for times—or simply contact a ranger while at Great Brook. In the winter the Great Brook Farm Ski Touring Center rents cross-country ski equipment.

The park is open year-round but is closed to mountain bikes from December 15 through March 15, or whenever more than four inches of snow blanket the ground. This allows cross-country skiing trails to remain intact as well as to keep erosion off Heart Break Ridge and other areas. The composition of the soil makes the landscape fairly fragile. When this ride was mapped in the early spring, several steep grades off the Ridge had signs warning of erosion and suggesting alternate routes.

If you can plan your ride to Great Brook Farm for late September or early October you'll be pleasantly greeted by an explosion of color. The foliage in this area makes fall an incredible time to venture out. A nice side-trip before or after your ride is to take a drive down Massachusetts 2 West and stop at a local farm stand. There are quite a few along the road and each has a sampling of local-grown vegetables, maple sugar candy, and other treats.

Ride Information

📞 Trail Contacts:
Great Brook Farm State Park, Carlisle, MA (978) 369-6312 • NEMBA, Acton, MA 1-800-57-NEMBA or *www.nemba.org*

🕐 Schedule:
Trail closed to mountain bikes from December 15 to March 15 or whenever there are four or more inches of snow on the ground.

❓ Local Information:
Carlisle Town Clerk, Carlisle, MA (978) 369-6155

🚲 Local Bike Shops:
Bikeway Cycles, Lexington, MA (781) 861-1199 • **Peter White Cycles,** Acton, MA (978) 635-0969 • **Belmont Wheel Works,** Belmont, MA (617) 489-3577

🅝 Maps:
USGS maps: Billerica, MA • Maps of the park are available at the map stand near the chicken coop.

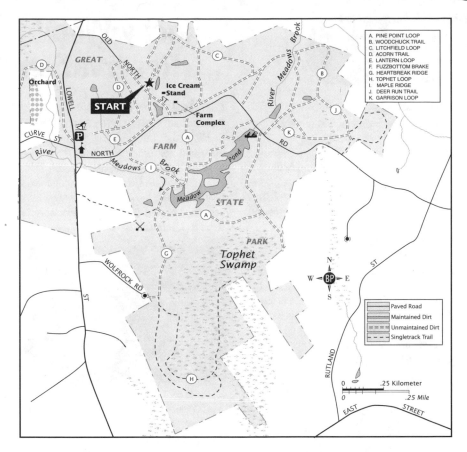

A. PINE POINT LOOP
B. WOODCHUCK TRAIL
C. LITCHFIELD LOOP
D. ACORN TRAIL
E. LANTERN LOOP
F. FUZZBOTTOM BRAKE
G. HEARTBREAK RIDGE
H. TOPHET LOOP
I. MAPLE RIDGE
J. DEER RUN TRAIL
K. GARRISON LOOP

Paved Road
Maintained Dirt
Unmaintained Dirt
Singletrack Trail

0   .25 Kilometer
0   .25 Mile

MilesDirections

Great Brook Farm offers many routes for most types of riders. The myriad paths suit beginners and intermediates, but advanced riders will find this area a little easy. To put together a seven-mile ride, begin at the chicken coop and head left up Litchfield Trail. This will act as a one-mile warm-up and will be suitable to challenge any beginner. Once you complete the loop, take a right on North Road and ride for about two-tenths of a mile. By taking a left into the woods here,

onto Maple Ridge, you'll run into a series of connected trails that will eventually bring you out at the canoe launching area.

This ride can be made more difficult by tackling Heart Break Ridge, a right-hand turn uphill off of Pine Point Loop at about one mile from where you turned onto Maple Ridge. As with any family riding area, remain aware of others on the trails and take care not to disturb equestrians.

24

Rocky Woods Reservation

Ride Specs

Start: From the park map next to the second fire gate in the Reservation

Length: 2.6-mile loop

Approximate Riding Time: 30 min.–1 hour

Difficulty Rating: An easy ride because of the mostly flat terrain and smooth bridle trails. Two very short sections might require beginners to walk because of rain ruts in a trail, but the rest is rideable.

Terrain: Entirely doubletrack bridle paths covered with wood chips or packed dirt. Two short sections that have loose rocks caused by water run-off. A number of medium-sized climbs with only a few short steep climbs.

Elevation Gain: 226 feet

Nearest Town: Medfield, MA

Other Trail Users: Hikers and equestrians

Getting There

From Boston: Take I-90 to I-95 South. Take I-95 South to MA 109 West (Exit 16B). Take MA 109 west for 5.7 miles. Take a right on Hartford Street in Medfield and follow it for about three miles. The Reservation entrance is on the right, and the parking area is next to the second fire gate. *DeLorme: Massachusetts Atlas & Gazetteer.* Page 52, C-9

Rocky Woods Reservation is a 500-acre tract of land owned and operated by the Trustees of Reservations (TOR), a private nonprofit conservation organization that helps protect over 20,000 acres of land on 78 reservations throughout Massachusetts. Founded in 1891 by landscape architect Charles Eliot, the TOR has grown to become a highly respected group of land conservation experts. Their efforts have helped to establish land trusts in England, Ireland, and other parts of the United States.

This private touch can be seen during your ride in the way the land is maintained. Volunteers and paid staff have laid large amounts of wood chips on the bridle trail to halt erosion and keep rain from causing trail damage. The ball field and picnic area at Rocky Woods are also well designed and cared for. Families make this park a frequent destination throughout the year.

In addition to the bridle paths, this park has an intertwined network of nature trails. Each path is well marked. The numbers at trailheads and intersections correspond with those in the guidebook for sale at the reservation visitor center. The book points out features of the land and the flora and fauna within the reservation while allowing you to tour the land at your own pace. With the large number of families and small children walking the nature trails, officials have prohibited mountain bikes from these areas.

While on your ride, take a moment to look at Echo Lake at about 0.4 miles. There is a long boardwalk across the center of the lake. It's an ideal place to take a photo. Other scenic spots include Chickering Lake, by the visitor center, and Whale Rock, which can be found by taking a right instead of a left at trail number 5.

If you enjoy sport fishing there are numbers of small fish in Chickering Lake, and fishing is allowed all year round. The only requirement is that you practice "catch and release." This means that you should use hooks without barbs and any fish you reel in must be returned to the lake. This allows the fish population to survive and help control the number of insects within the reservation.

On the subject of bugs, be sure to bring some spray because the number of small ponds creates a prime breeding ground for mosquitoes. Ticks are less of a problem here because the trails are wide and foliage seldom comes in contact with your body. In fact, with the doubletrack dirt trails the only thing you might find sticking to your legs is mud from the infrequent puddles.

If you're just starting out in this sport, but need more than a parking lot to stimulate you, Rocky Woods is a great place to spread your wings. This ride offers some challenges with instant rewards and the surroundings are a great introduction to the outdoors. The distance is not difficult, and if riders want to extend the ride they can double the loop or do this ride backwards after riding it once.

Ride Information

◉ Trail Contacts:
Rocky Woods Reservation, Medfield, MA c/o Trustees of Reservations (508) 785-0339 or *www.thetrustees.org*

⑤ Fees/Permits:
There is no cost but you must be a Trustees of Reservations member or have a mountain bike pass to ride in this park. For a mountain bike pass or to become a TOR member call the general headquarters at (978) 921-1944.

◉ Schedule:
The park is open year-round, sunrise to sunset, but it is closed to mountain bikes March 1 through April 30.

❓ Local Information:
South Shore Chamber of Commerce, Quincy, MA (617) 479-1111 • **Metro South Chamber of Commerce,** Brockton, MA (508) 586-0500

◉ Local Events/Attractions:
Dedham Historical Society, Dedham, MA (781) 326-1385 • **Marino Lookout Farm**, South Natick, MA (508) 655-2248

◉ Other Resources:
A Reservation guidebook, produced by the TOR is available on weekends at the visitor center or by calling (978) 921-1944.

◉ Local Bike Shops:
Town & Country Bicycles, Medfield, MA (508) 359-8377 • **Harris Cyclery**, West Newton, MA (617) 244-1040 • **International Bicycle**, Newton, MA (617) 527-0967

◉ Maps:
USGS maps: Medfield, MA • A map is displayed right next to the main parking area for reference. Purchase one at the visitor center on weekends for $2.

MilesDirections

Trails are marked at intersections with numbers nailed to trees. Some signs also have names.

0.0 START riding to the right on the wood chip-covered bridle trail while facing the trail map at the main parking area.

0.1 Take a left on the Loop Trail.

0.3 Take a right on TR 16, "Echo Lake."

0.6 Go right at TR 15.

0.7 Go left at the "Y" intersection of TR 14.

0.8 Take a left at TR 13.

1.0 Ride to the right at TR 12.

1.1 Go right at TR 11.

1.2 At the "Y" intersection at TR 8 go left. Stay left as you come up quickly to another "Y" intersection.

1.7 Take a right onto TR 6.

1.8 Take a left at TR 5. Follow this down a harder, rocky descent.

2.2 Go right at TR 2 and then take a left at TR 3.

2.4 Follow TR 3 as it takes a sharp right uphill around a reservation building and then down into the ball field. Continue straight on this trail as it turns from grass back into wood chips.

2.6 Return to the reservation map and the parking area.

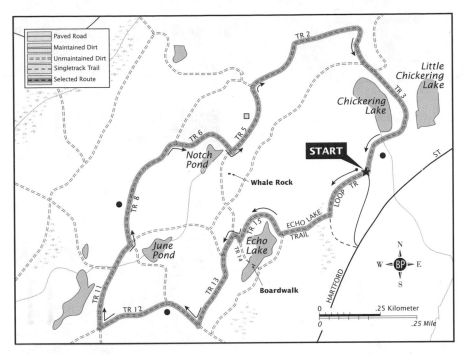

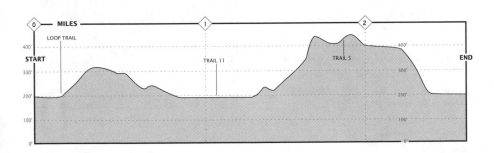

Purgatory Chasm
State Reservation

Ride Specs

Start: From the last parking area on the left of Purgatory Road
Length: 3 miles of trail within 900 acres
Difficulty Rating: The trails in this ride are moderate to difficult because the trail changes drastically from smooth dirt to one with boulders the size of laundry baskets.
Terrain: Dirt doubletrack fire roads, technical singletrack with roots and large rocks, paved access roads, and a minor portion of slickrock
Nearest Town: Sutton, MA
Other Trail Users: Hikers, family groups walking around and above the Chasm, and rock-climbers

Getting There

From Boston: Take I-90 West to Worcester and MA 146 (Exit 10A). Take MA South and travel southeast toward the town of Sutton. Purgatory Chasm State Reservation is on the right side and is accessed by Purgatory Road. Drive to the last parking area on the left to begin the ride. *DeLorme: Massachusetts Atlas & Gazetteer.* Page 50, H-13

urgatory is not at all what the name connotes. According to the American Heritage Dictionary purgatory is a place or condition of suffering. Purgatory Chasm can offer suffering in the way of difficult descents and large obstacles, but overall it's a pleasant little park that has been groomed for family use. With picnic tables, a covered pavilion, restrooms, plentiful parking, and a number of short hiking/biking loops, it's a great place to visit when you have a half-day to spend relaxing. During the summer the ice cream man makes a regular stop by the pavilion in case you forgot to bring lunch.

Additional features that make the park popular are the playing field on the other side of the road across from the Chasm and the scenic rock walls within the Chasm. Formed thousands of years ago from the sudden release of glacial meltwater, the Chasm was left behind with walls of granite reaching 70 feet and running for a length of three-tenths of a mile. This makes for a stunning picture, and if you're interested, a thrilling climb. Although bikes are not allowed in the Chasm, the view is worth the short hike.

Formed in 1919, Purgatory Chasm State Reservation comprises 900 acres, with gifts of land having come from many fronts. Of the reserve's 187 acres of forest, the marked

trails and roads only touch a modest portion. The hiking trails within the reserve form two large loops, with a number of shorter, one-way trails that lead to the edge of the Chasm. Each spoke, or short trail, leads to a scenic overlook into the Chasm, and each has a peculiar name, like Fat Man's Misery or Devil's Corncrib. The overlook at each is quite high, and there are sad stories of people having died after leaping or falling into the Chasm. So be careful.

Riding in Purgatory Chasm will no doubt challenge your bike handling and test your ability to stop on a dime. Since your riding is primarily on hiking trails, children are often seen darting about. These added obstacles are probably a benefit because they keep intelligent riders from bombing down trails that often end with sharp turns or monstrous rocks. At any time you are fairly close to the main road, so Purgatory makes a good next step for riders who have mastered carriage paths and paved bike trails.

Aside from Purgatory Chasm, the town of Sutton's main claim to fame is hosting a Professional Golfers Association (PGA) tournament. The CVS Charity Classic used to be held at Pleasant Valley Country Club. This private golf course has been home to a PGA event since 1965. Unfortunately, Pleasant Valley hosted its last men's event in 1998. Because of scheduling conflicts, the PGA Tour has eliminated this stop on the tour. Luckily, the LPGA (the women's league) has picked up the slack and will play at least one event in Sutton each year.

The golf course at Pleasant Valley was created from apple orchards and abutting land in 1961 by Cosmo Mingolla. Mingolla had been involved in designing bridges and highways, but felt that the region needed a top-notch golf course. He set about creating Pleasant Valley Country Club. Mingolla died in 1979, but his course lives on under the guidance of his son, Edward Mingolla. The younger Mingolla added a beneficial twist to the Pleasant Valley tradition by turning each PGA tournament held at the course into a charitable event. The American Lung Association, United Way, Boys & Girls Clubs, Easter Seals, and others have all benefited generously from Pleasant Valley. If you'd like to watch the professionals tee it up, make your trip to Sutton in mid summer. The pro-am is usually free. On other tournament days the fees to watch are reasonable.

If you'd like to watch nature instead, head back to Purgatory. With this purgatory you'll be glad you went.

Ride Information

🍃 Trail Contacts:
Purgatory Chasm Visitor's Center, Sutton, MA (508) 234-3733 • **NEMBA**, Acton, MA 1-800-57-NEMBA or www.nemba.org

🕐 Schedule:
The reservation is open year-round from sunrise to sunset.

❓ Local Information:
Worcester County Convention & Visitor's Bureau, Worcester, MA (508) 753-2920 or (508) 755-7400 • **Sutton Town Clerk**, Sutton, MA (508) 865-8725

💡 Local Events/Attractions:
Climbing permits are available at Forest Headquarters. They are free and available from May 1 through November 30. Rangers will inspect your gear before issuing a permit. • **Pleasant Valley Country Club Tournament Office,** Sutton, MA (508) 865-1491

🚲 Local Bike Shops:
Fritz's Bicycle & Fitness, Worcester, MA (508) 853-1799 – *offers bicycle repair classes* • **O'Neil's Bicycle & Ski Shop,** Worcester, MA (508) 798-0084

Ⓝ Maps:
USGS maps: Milford, MA; Uxbridge, MA • Trail maps are available at the Visitor Center and beside the Pavilion at the entrance to the Chasm.

MilesDirections

Purgatory Chasm, when viewed on a map, is shaped like a football. This is convenient when riding around the Chasm because each side has one main path. Off of each main path are a number of smaller paths that dead end at the Chasm, giving you a great chance to photograph this natural phenomenon. To make this into a longer ride, start at the main end of the "football" and ride either side to the opposite end. From there, pick up a fire road which will lead you deeper into the reservation. By taking right turns at every major intersection you'll end up on the main access road to the Chasm.

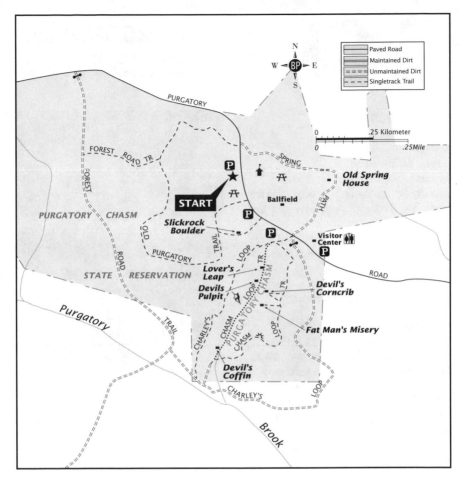

26

Leominster State Forest

Ride Specs

Start: From the dirt parking area at the entrance to Rocky Pond Road
Length: 7.8-mile circuit
Approximate Riding Time: 1–1½ hours
Difficulty Rating: Moderate. Though all on fire roads, it gets thin in some areas and has some brutal climbs and hairy descents.
Terrain: Dirt doubletrack fire roads with some imbedded rocks and loose gravel surfaces
Elevation Gain: 628 feet
Nearest Town: Westminster, MA
Other Trail Users: Hikers and equestrians

Getting There

From Boston: Travel west on MA 2 to Fitchburg and MA 31 South (Exit 28). Go south on MA 31 for a few miles, past the Forest Headquarters and the two main parking areas. Take a left on Rocky Pond Road, which immediately becomes a dirt parking area. *DeLorme: Massachusetts Atlas & Gazetteer.* Page 26, O-4

L eominster State Forest spreads itself out over five towns, has over 4,000 acres, and offers some fairly dramatic elevation changes in short stretches of trail. For example, during this ride the highest point is about 1,000 feet. Less than a mile away from it you'll at be about 700 feet elevation. The hills are lined with many species of trees and brush including oak, elm, and birch trees as well as mountain laurel and ferns. This vegetation makes the tops of the climbs, as well as the climbs themselves, very scenic.

Beyond the views, Leominster offers a great deal to the recreational visitor. During the summer Crow Hill Pond is open for swimming. The extensive hiking trail system explores even more of the park than you can see on this ride. A group of mountain bikers have been helping to maintain the hiking trails with the hope of one day having the vast network opened up to cyclists. Currently riders who are found on the hiking trails receive a warning from the forest rangers who also have the authority to issue fines and arrest violators.

This fire road trail can be a four-season ride, but in the winter and fall, the forest is open to hunting and snowmobiling. Hunters can be more easily avoided by paying attention to the hunting season and by biking on Sundays. The same trails open to bik-

ing and horseback riding are also open to the snowmobiles, so stay alert. Cross-country skiing is allowed on the hiking trails as are snowshoeing and winter hiking.

There are abundant ponds and streams in the Leominster area and many are packed with fish. All you need to enjoy a day of angling is a permit and a fishing rod. Fishing conditions depend on each individual pond or stream and the weather. Some ponds are too shallow for fish to survive, as the summer sun is able to heat the small volume of water. Be sure to ask which ponds are best when you purchase your permit.

For a more active pursuit, the Wachusett Ski Area is a short drive away and offers both day and night skiing for reasonable lift ticket fees. If you've never skied at night, it can be compared to mountain biking at night. The surface of the slopes becomes flatter because of the artificial lights, and your reflexes play a larger role in making it down the slope without falling. Also, when skiing at night, be sure to bundle up because weather conditions are generally more extreme than in the day.

In addition to being a great mountain biking locale, Leominster is home to the National Plastics Center and Museum. The center is housed in an old schoolhouse that dates to 1913. Hands-on exhibits, a plastics hall of fame, and chemistry demonstrations are just a few of the things you'll see. It takes at least an hour to see properly.

This ride is mainly a test of stamina, though some parts of it are tricky enough to toss you to the ground if you're not paying attention. Fire roads offer the challenge of maneuvering your bike at high speeds on slightly uneven surfaces and enduring long drawn-out climbs.

Ride Information

📞 Trail Contacts:
Leominster State Forest, Leominster, MA (978) 874-2303 • **NEMBA**, Acton, MA 1-800-57-NEMBA or *www.nemba.org*

☀ Schedule:
The forest is open year-round for visitors. Riding is allowed only on unpaved roads.

❓ Local Information:
Leominster Area Chamber of Commerce, Leominster, MA (978) 840-4300

💡 Local Events/Attractions:
National Plastics Center and Museum, Leominster, MA (978) 537-9529 • **Wachusett Ski Area**, Princeton, MA (978) 464-2300

🔧 Local Bike Shops:
Gamache Cyclery, Inc., Fitchburg, MA (978) 343-3140 • **O'Neils Bicycle Shop**, Leominster, MA (978) 537-6464

🗺 Maps:
USGS maps: Fitchburg, MA • Forest maps are available at the Forest Headquarters on the right side of Massachusetts 31 as you drive toward the parking area.

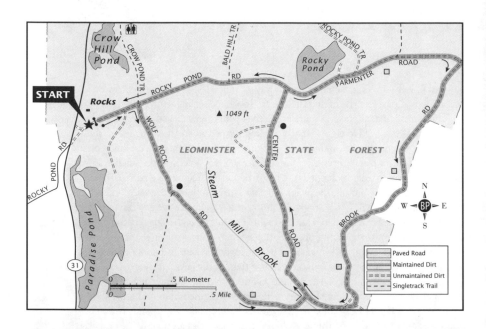

MilesDirections

0.0 START from the bottom of the parking lot at the fire gate entrance to Rocky Pond Road. This is a fire road that immediately climbs slightly and has a loose, rocky surface.

0.3 Take a right on Wolf Rock Road, a fire road with a moderate slope to it.

0.7 At the "Y" in the trail stay left on Wolf Rock Road.

1.7 After a steep and fast downhill section take a left on Center Road.

2.8 Take a right onto Parmenter Road at the "T" intersection with Rocky Pond and Parmenter Road.

3.7 Take a right at the four-way intersection onto Brook Road.

5.4 Take a right onto Center Road again.

5.7 Wolf Rock Road is to the left, continue straight on Center Road.

6.8 Take a left onto Rocky Pond Road at the "T" intersection with Rocky Pond and Parmenter Road.

7.6 Continue straight on Rocky Pond Road as Wolf Rock Road goes left.

7.8 Finish the ride at the fire gate and the dirt parking area.

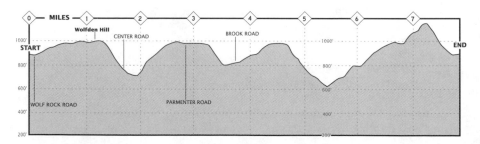

138

Upton State Forest **27**

Ride Specs

Start: From the parking lot at the end of Loop Road. (This road is next to the entrance to the Forest Headquarters and is a dirt fire road.)
Length: 6.4-mile loop
Approximate Riding Time: 1–1½ hours
Difficulty Rating: Mostly moderate with one short section that would prove difficult even for professional riders
Terrain: Soft, loamy singletrack, packed dirt, and loose gravel doubletrack with some wicked rooty sections and hard, rock-strewn fire roads
Elevation Gain: 616 feet
Nearest Town: Upton, MA
Other Trail Users: Hikers, equestrians, and the Armed Forces

Getting There

From Boston: Take I-90 East to MA 495. Take MA 495 South toward Upton to MA 135 (Exit 21B). Go west on MA 135 to Westboro Road, which is on the left. Take Westboro Road to Spring Street. Turn right onto Spring Street and then almost immediately turn right onto a dirt fire road that leads to the Upton State Forest parking area. Park anywhere in this lot.
DeLorme: Massachusetts Atlas & Gazetteer: Page 51, C-19

A large portion of this ride is on fairly new trails. The surface feels like a sponge because the dirt has not been packed down by years of trail use. Additionally, the stumps in the trail have not been worn down to the ground by tires or horse hooves. These conditions make riding a little taxing because each pedal stroke loses some power to the soft, cushioned path. These conditions also contribute a little danger as the three to five-inch stumps can stop or deflect a front wheel in an instant making a rider's next move quite crucial.

Riding downhill is also a challenge because the soft surface is also a little loose, making braking less effective. But the downhills are mostly moderate in slope and have long areas to run out if the bike begins to get out of control. One area, at the end of Whistling Cave Trail, has a steep climb that's fairly impossible to finish. Riding it the other way is even more difficult. The broken reflectors and scratched tree stumps at the bottom of the hill are silent witnesses.

Some not-so-silent forest dwellers are the motorcycle riders who occasionally buzz down the doubletrack and wide singletrack trails. Although the regulations prohibit motorized vehicles, it's wise to keep an ear cocked when crossing the fire roads or riding around blind corners. Some motorcycle riders are oblivious to their surroundings and may scream past without even a nod—but most are courteous.

Another bunch you may see leaving the forest as you arrive is the Army. By the time most cyclists arrive, at about 9 a.m. or 10 a.m. on a weekend, these reservists have

Ride Information

📞 Trail Contacts:
Upton State Forest, Upton, MA (508) 529-6923 • **NEMBA**, Acton, MA 1-800-57-NEMBA or *www.nemba.org*

🕐 Schedule:
The park is open year-round. Hunting is allowed so ride on Sundays or wear blaze orange during hunting season.

🍸 Local Bike Shops:
Fritz's Bicycle Shop, Worcester, MA (508) 853-1799 • **O'Neil's Bicycle & Ski Shop**, Worcester, MA (508) 798-0084

Ⓝ Maps:
USGS maps: Milford, MA • Trail maps are available at the parking lot in the map box.

MilesDirections

0.0 START the ride from the dirt parking lot near the map case. Keep the fire gate at your back and the map on your right and begin riding down the doubletrack fire road, Loop Road, toward the street.

0.1 Take a right on Spring Street and an immediate left into the woods at the blue marker. This singletrack trail winds through the forest for about three miles while crossing a few paved roads.

0.2 Cross Westboro Road and continue on the singletrack trail.

0.3 Cross Ridge Road onto Rabbit Run Trail, a singletrack path that climbs up into the woods.

1.5 Take a left on a short section of doubletrack that leads back to Ridge Road. Cross the road and enter the singletrack trail as it continues climbing.

1.8 Cross Westboro Road again and ride onto Old Hopkinton Spring Trail. This singletrack cruises up and down through the woods with two steep descents and one long climb.

2.3 At the "Y" intersection, stay left on Old Hopkinton.

2.4 At the "T" intersection, take a right on wide singletrack.

2.7 Take a right onto a doubletrack trail at the "Trail" sign.

3.0 Take a left into the woods at the "Trail" sign. This singletrack has one mean downhill that drops onto Spring Street.

3.2 Cross over Spring Street and head right for a moment, then take a left back into the forest on Mammoth Rock Trail.

3.9 At the "Y" intersection Mammoth Rock Trail is the right-hand section. Stay to the right.

4.2 At the intersection with Grouse Trail, go straight over the rock wall down to Loop Road, a dirt fire road.

4.21 Take a left on Loop Road.

4.4 Take a right up a wicked doubletrack uphill—this is Hawk Trail.

4.8 Take a left off of Hawk Trail onto Middle Road, also a dirt doubletrack.

5.1 Take a right onto Whistling Cave Trail. This singletrack trail has lots of roots and ends with a steep climb.

5.8 Come to a "T" intersection with doubletrack fire road, Park Road. Take a right.

6.3 Go left onto Loop Road.

6.4 Cross through the fire gate at the dirt parking lot to end the ride.

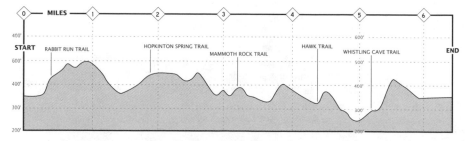

already jogged through the woods and accomplished all their soldiering for the day. One bonus to arriving while the troops are still at Upton is that they bring along their own port-o-potties. They're cleaner than the ones typically found at a concert or football game, and the army personnel are kind enough to let riders change or relieve themselves inside.

This ride can become wet in a few spots, but for the most part, it's high enough that water drains off the trail. In one spot at the beginning of Old Hopkinton Spring Trail, there's a small river that crosses the singletrack at the base of a large uphill, but at the time of publishing, a bridge was being built to span the crossing. The other wet spots are on Whistling Cave Trail, before the uphill and at the very start of this ride as it enters the forest off of Spring Street.

Because of the unused trails and broad variety of terrain, the future of Upton State Forest looks bright. The paths are easy to follow and getting lost isn't usually a problem as there are many fire roads that cross through the woods and lead back to paved residential streets. A final suggestion is to take care on the tricky sections and bring some tires that grip well on loose surfaces—at least until this trail sees another season or two of riders.

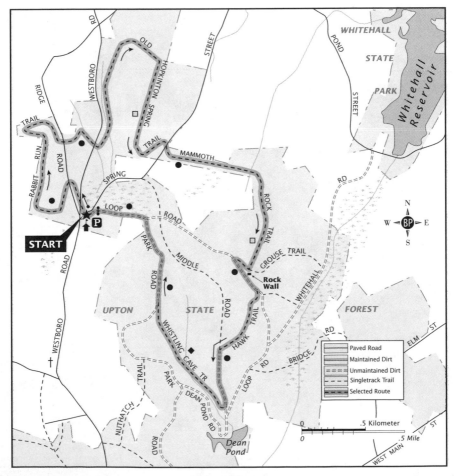

Cape Cod

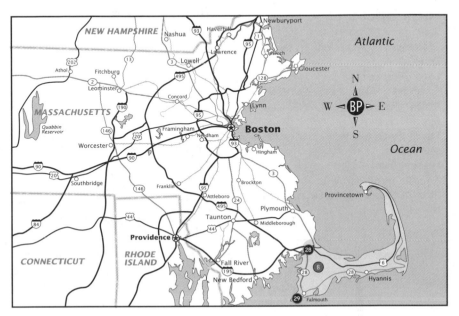

The Cape is a breed all its own. The terrain is fast, buffed singletrack with many short, steep hills and some rocks and roots. The sand here will toss your bike sideways and make riding extremely difficult, but the sand can be avoided and is sometimes a great test of handling skills.

The scenery on the Cape is unmatched. Green or deep blue water and sand dunes that seem to shift before your eyes are just part of the sights. Both the Canal ride and the Shining Sea Bikeway offer ample opportunity to stop and look around. Spending some time on the Cape in the fall or spring is precious because there are fewer tourists, and you'll be able to still enjoy moderate temperatures and blooming or turning foliage. The best part is that the Cape is less than an hour from Boston.

Cape Cod Canal

Ride Specs

Start: From the recreation area parking lot underneath the Cape side of the Bourne Bridge

Length: 9.5-mile circuit

Approximate Riding Time: ¾–1¼ hours

Difficulty Rating: Easy to Moderate due to the wind and distance

Terrain: Paved bike paths, main roads, and sidewalks

Elevation Gain: 375 feet

Nearest Town: Bourne, MA

Other Trail Users: Joggers, in-line skaters, and anglers

Getting There

From Boston: Take I-93 South to MA 3 South (Exit 7). Take MA 3 South to the end at the Sagamore Bridge. MA 6 begins as you continue straight and cross over the Sagamore Bridge. Take Exit 1 off of MA 6. Follow it to the end, a "T" intersection with MA 6A. Take a left onto MA 6A and follow this road to the Bourne Recreation Area, which is on the right. *DeLorme: Massachusetts Atlas & Gazetteer.* Page 65, A-20

> The width of Cape Cod goes from about 20 miles at its base to a few hundred yards at the tip.

The Cape Cod Canal is the world's widest sea-level canal with a minimum bottom width of 480 feet and a controlling depth of 32 feet at low tide. The canal is 17.4 miles in length. Along both sides, of the Cape and of the mainland, there are paved paths for biking and other recreational activities. This ride covers area on both sides of the canal and affords riders two perspectives of this amazing waterway.

The canal was only 100-feet wide and 15-feet deep when it was created in 1914 by August Belmont (he also created the Belmont horse track and helped build a number of bridges in New York). Swift currents in the canal caused many accidents, and as a result, a number of ship captains reverted back to taking the long way around the Cape. It took a decade and a half before the government, in 1928, stepped in and presented the canal project to the Army Corps of Engineers. The Corps' assignment was to make the waterway safe and to control the traffic traveling through the canal.

During this ride you may see any number of different boats motoring through the water beside you. The key word here is motoring. The strong tides and fast-moving water in the canal make sailing dangerous, Sailboats are only allowed through under engine power.

The strong tides and deep waters make the canal an ideal place to fish, and many people have outfitted their bikes for this purpose. Some people even have attached fishing pole holders to the sides of their frame so that they can travel up and down the canal easily in search of fish. People tend to catch striped bass and bluefish, as well as an occasional herring.

Spanning the waterway in two locations, about three miles apart, are two large bridges. Each was started in 1935 and finished in 1955 and was built high enough for the largest ocean liner to travel underneath. When crossing these 135-foot high structures it is recommended that riders dismount and walk their bikes. This is because the

winds at the top of the bridge are pretty strong and running into the steel fence or falling off the two-foot high curb into traffic would be painful.

From the west bank looking across the water riders can see other trail users and a vast array of greenery. Trees belie the fact that both shores are fairly well developed. The structures are just more hidden on the east bank. When riding down the east bank houses can be seen dotting the shoreline, and the road is visible in a few places. The landscape is much higher on the west bank and the sandy hills provide a nice backdrop for photos of the majestic houses perched on top.

The only trail hazards are the wind, which whistles through the canal and can stop your bike in its tracks, and the clam shells scattered along the pavement. The broken shells are actually dropped by over-flying seagulls. Overall this is a beautiful ride, offering some great scenery and a glimpse into how man sometimes succeeds when he tries to control nature.

MilesDirections

0.0 START the ride at the ranger station in the Bourne Recreation Area, under the Bourne Bridge on the Cape side of the canal. Keep the canal at your back and ride out to the access road to the recreation area, Sandwich Road.

0.1 Take a right on Sandwich Road.

0.3 Take a left on Veteran's Road.

0.4 Take a left through the State Police parking lot and to the base of the Bourne Bridge.

0.5 Ride onto the Bourne Bridge sidewalk.

1.2 On the other side of the bridge, take a left behind the hotel and through the parking lot to Massachusetts 6.

1.3 Take a left onto Massachusetts 6 and follow it under the Bourne Bridge.

1.4 Take a right into the Bourne Scenic Park camping area. Ride to the back of the park, which is next to West Canal Service Road.

1.7 Ride left onto the path beside the Cape Cod Canal, West Canal Service Road.

4.8 At the "Y" in the path, take a left onto the Parking Access up the hill and under the Sagamore Bridge. Ride straight into the Sagamore Recreation Area.

5.0 Take a left out of the recreation area onto Canal Road. Stay on the left sidewalk and follow the road up to Friendly's Restaurant.

5.1 Follow the sidewalk left as it turns toward the Sagamore Bridge.

5.2 Ride onto the Sagamore Bridge sidewalk.

5.8 At the other side of the bridge turn left into the Christmas Tree Shop parking lot. Stay left and go to the other side of the lot.

5.9 Ride left down the Christmas Tree Shop driveway to a "T" intersection with Massachusetts 6A.

6.0 Take a left onto Massachusetts 6A and then a right after about 60 yards at the edge of the Sagamore Bridge. Ride through this dirt parking lot across the train tracks and onto East Canal Service Road.

6.2 Take a left on East Canal Service Road and follow it down the east side of the canal.

9.4 Take a left at the Bourne Recreation Area, over the train tracks and into the parking area.

9.5 End the ride at the ranger station.

Ride Information

🕭 Trail Contacts:
Cape Cod Canal Recreation Hotline, Buzzards Bay, MA (508) 759-5991

🕐 Schedule:
The area is open year-round. Ranger stations have varied hours.

❓ Local Information:
Cape Cod Canal Region Chamber of Commerce, Buzzards Bay, MA (508) 759-6000

📍 Local Events/Attractions:
Aptucxet Trading Post Museum, Buzzards Bay, MA (508) 759-9487 • **Heritage Plantation Sandwich,** MA

(508) 888-3300 – *open May through October* • **Sandwich Glass Museum,** Sandwich, MA (508) 888-0251

🚲 Local Bike Shops:
P & M Cycles, Buzzards Bay, MA (508) 759-2830 • **Cape Cod Bike Rental/Sandwich Cycles,** Sandwich, MA (508) 833-2453 • **Village Cycles,** Buzzards Bay, MA (508) 759-6773

Ⓝ Maps:
USGS maps: Sagamore, MA; Pocasset, MA • Canal maps are available at the Recreation Areas at either end of the canal.

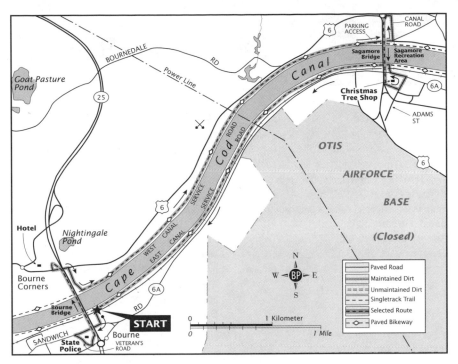

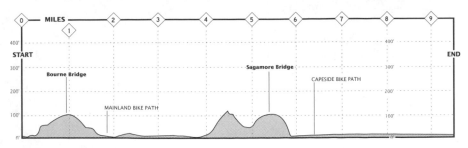

Shining Sea Bikeway

Ride Specs

Start: From Falmouth Town Hall facing Main Street
Length: 7.9-mile out-and-back
Approximate Riding Time: ¾–1½ hours
Difficulty Rating: Easy
Terrain: Paved roads and a well-maintained paved bike path
Nearest Town: Falmouth, MA
Elevation Gain: 222 feet
Other Trail Users: Walkers, in-line skaters, and joggers

Getting There

From Boston: Take I-93 South to MA 3 South (Exit 7). Take MA 3 South to the end at the Sagamore Bridge. MA 6 begins as you continue straight and cross over the Sagamore Bridge. Take Exit 1 off of MA 6. Follow it to the end, a "T" intersection with MA 6A. Take a left onto MA 6A and follow it to MA 28 South. Head south on MA 28 to Falmouth, MA. As you enter town MA 28 changes its name to Palmer Avenue. Follow MA 28 as it turns left onto West Main Street. Shortly thereafter, take a right into the Falmouth Town Hall parking lot.
DeLorme: Massachusetts Atlas & Gazetteer. Page 65, L-18

The Shining Sea Bikeway is a community project, meaning it has been organized and created by the town for the benefit of residents and visitors. It was dedicated in 1975, but there are new sections still being added to the path, making it even longer. Right now the Bikeway winds through Falmouth toward the ferry terminal at Woods Hole. This paved trail, the only bike path along the Cape, offers great views of the open ocean. In fact, on a clear day you can see Martha's Vineyard, which sits about a mile off the coast. The path was originally a route that the Wampanoag Indians took from their village to the ocean. The surrounding land and ponds are a feeding ground for waterfowl and deer—which is likely the reason the Native Americans remained here. It was also along this trail that the Pilgrims received their first greeting when they came to America. The Wampanoag Chief made first contact with the group in 1620 as they made their way up to Plymouth.

Later on, the pathway was turned into a railway for trains coming from as far away as New York. The steam-powered locomotives carried everything from people to coal and helped spark the burgeoning tourist center that the Cape is today. Running from the late 1800s to 1959, the trains also brought seafood from the Cape to towns and cities far inland.

Along this trail are over 20 acres of woods, ponds, swamps, and marshes. This is a superb place to bring a camera. The south-facing beaches make the water slightly warmer than the regular ice-like temperatures found elsewhere on the Cape. Counter balancing this positive is the fact that this part of the coast is a prime target for ocean storms. Notice the houses on the left as you ride toward Woods Hole. They've been built on large pilings so that surging water can pass harmlessly underneath them during a hurricane.

The Shining Sea Bikeway, if looked at in terms of terrain and trail features, would be boring. But when looked at as a winding bike path that dips near beaches and marshes while twisting down to Woods Hole, it's fantastic. The elevation change on this ride is minimal and it is unlikely to tax your muscles. What will be taxed are your senses as you see birds, flora, seascapes, and many more stunning examples of New England scenery.

At the entrance to the bikeway is a large chunk of granite with a woman's name engraved in it. This woman, Katherine Lee Bates, was raised in Falmouth and used to write poetry here in the late 1800s. Her poem "America The Beautiful" was set to music by Samuel Ward and is now the most sung song in the United States. It's last line reads: "And crown thy good with brotherhood, from sea to shining sea." Enjoy the ride along this shining sea.

Ride Information

🕭 Trail Contacts:
The path is along paved roads and a bike path, so there is no trail contact.

🕙 Schedule:
Open year-round. The rules of the road apply on the path—keep right and step off the path if you stop.

❓ Local Information:
Falmouth Chamber of Commerce, Falmouth, MA (508) 548-8500

🔾 Local Events/Attractions:
Nobska Light, on Church Street, Falmouth, MA – *a famous lighthouse in Woods Hole with views of the coast* • **The Village Green**, on Main Street, Falmouth, MA – *This spot was once used to train militia.* • **The Congregational Church**, on the Green, Falmouth, MA – *has a bell in it made by Paul Revere* • **The Falmouth Road Race**, 3rd Sunday in August, Falmouth, MA – *run through the streets of the town*

🚲 Local Bike Shops:
Bicycle Zone, East Falmouth, MA (508) 540-2453 • **Art's Bike Shop**, North Falmouth, MA (508) 563-7379 • **Corner Cycle**, Falmouth, MA (508) 540-4195

Ⓝ Maps:
USGS maps: Falmouth, MA; Woods Hole, MA • Maps are available at the entrance to the Bikeway. An extension to the trail is currently under construction.

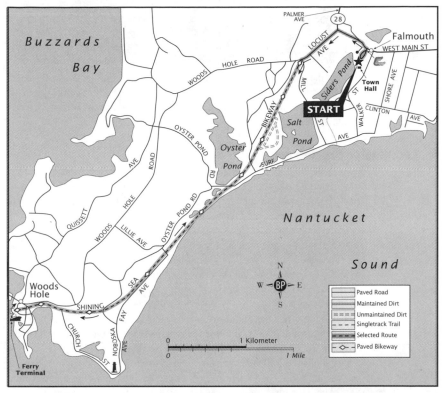

MilesDirections

0.0 START by facing West Main Street with the Falmouth Town Hall behind you. Take a left onto West Main Street.

0.1 Stay to the left at the "Y" intersection.

0.3 Take a left onto Locust Avenue. Ride on the right side of the road.

0.7 Enter the Shining Sea Bikeway at the granite stone and welcome map.

3.3 At the parking lot for the island ferry, continue straight and follow the bike lane to the terminal building.

3.9 Enjoy the view of Martha's Vineyard and the water. From here you can board a ferry to the Vineyard for about $10 one-way with your bike. But to continue this ride, turn around and head back into the ferry parking lot.

7.3 Turn right onto Locust Avenue north.

7.6 Take a right onto West Main Street.

7.9 Finish the ride with a right turn into the Falmouth Town Hall parking lot.

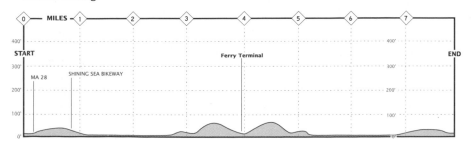

Honorable Mentions

Noted below are a few of the great rides in the Greater Boston area that didn't make the A-list this time around but deserve recognition nonetheless. Check them out and let us know what you think. You may decide that they deserve higher status in future editions or, perhaps, you may have a ride of your own that merits some attention. Just let us know.

(A) Leominster Singletrack

This is great New England singletrack. This trail system has been worked on recently by NEMBA members and others and soon may be entirely legal. Until it is, it'll have to be an honorable mention. Right now there are informal rides here every week. The entrance is near the Leominster State Forest ride.

Leominster has many short climbs and winding switchbacks. The trails are littered with rocks and roots and technical prowess is valued here. While riding here you'll see many varieties of trees, wildlife, and terrain. The pine needles and leaves can obscure some parts of the trail, but they make crashing less painful. Some climbs here are very difficult, but are rewarded with winding, looping singletrack through the trees on fairly smooth dirt.

There are plenty of rocks and roots but very few impossible ledges or drop-offs. The trail system crosses over itself in many places making ride choices easy. The forest can remain wet in areas so bring bug repellant and mud tires.

Get a local rider on NEMBA's website or on a New England mountain biking list to show you the trails. The labyrinth of trails can be very confusing and having a guide who's familiar with the area will only increase the amount of fun you can have. Bring lunch because it's a 15-minute drive to a restaurant or fast food place.

(B) Stow Forest

Stow Forest is a community owned recreational area that lacks organized trail enforcement. It's legal to bike here, but the Stow Conservation Commission would rather not promote that fact. Mountain bikers could do well to assemble and show a positive force in this area before the land managers decide to ban biking. It's out of respect to the Stow Conservation Commission that we make mention of this area only as an honorable mention and encourage mountain bikers to be respectful of the land while here.

The forest is an intertwined mass of singletrack, doubletrack, and fire roads, as well as an area with some sandy clearings and grass meadows. The trails are essentially unmarked but getting lost isn't a problem as houses and water border the woods. With approximately 1,000 acres of trails in the woods, loops can be made as short as two miles or as long as 10 or 15. A loop of six miles can be pieced together with minimal sections of overlapping trail. Be aware that motorcycles use these trails. And please, steer clear of private property.

At the back of the dirt parking lot there are two openings. One leads through a fire gate to a ball field and the other leads between towering trees onto the mountain bike trail. The ride begins with a short drop down a rocky section then immediately mellows as the path turns into doubletrack and goes for about a half-mile before entering the woods on semi-technical singletrack.

From this point riders can link up with loops that come into the trail from both sides by alternating between left and right turns. The trails that intersect the main singletrack either loop back to the beginning, dead-end at the ball field or swamp, or hook around ahead of the main trail. In the first few minutes, off-camber riding and fast weaving trails are an unexpected treat. Also unexpected are the number of mosquitoes you'll find in the woods. This ride has water on many sides making bug repellent a must. The worst areas are at the tops of the hills and on the trails that run alongside the streams and swamps.

You'll find Stow Forest off of Massachusetts 117 at the end Bradley Lane in the town of Stow. To see how you as a mountain biker can help curry favor with the Stow Conservation Commission, contact them at (978) 897-8615. They can also help you out with maps to the area.

Ⓒ Otis

Located just south of the Cape Cod Canal ride, Otis is owned by the U.S. Air Force and is not considered "officially" legal, so we're demoting it to an honorable mention. There seems to be little fear that the Air Force will develop this riding area, but to keep on the good side of the Air Force, stay off the base and away from the homes that are on the base. You'll know you made a wrong turn if you can see houses from the trail.

Otis is a lung-busting, leg-testing, fast, and fun trail. Where some rides punish you before rewarding you, Otis lets minimal effort result in maximum pleasure. The problem with a ride this fun is that you just keep going farther away from where you parked. Before you know it your car is 20 miles away and you're dead tired. One section of the ride, which is representative of the entire trail system, begins with a 100-yard downhill. It then turns into a banked right-hand turn and then climbs for 60 yards and plateaus before heading downhill again. This continues for as far as you can see.

Singletrack with roots, imbedded rocks, and sand in places is what you can expect. The trails drain well because of the sandy base, but be careful coming downhill into a patch of sand-bikes handle differently when pedaled through four inches of sand. Most of the trail is smooth and buffed hard dirt.

Bring 2.0 or higher tires if it's been a dry season. These will help you ride on top of the sandy areas. Also, bring a computer. The main trail next to Massachusetts 28 is an out-and-back path. Check your computer regularly and turn around before you get tired. Pushing your bike up 60-yard hills is a pain. The nearest bathroom is at the veterinarian's office. Closest food is just over the Bourne Bridge at the rotary.

Bicycle Clubs and Organizations

National Clubs and Organizations

American Trails
The only national, nonprofit organization working on behalf of ALL trail interests. Members want to create and protect America's network of interconnected trailways.
POB 200787, Denver, CO 80220
(303) 321-6606, *www.outdoorlink.com/amtrails*

International Mountain Bicycling Association (IMBA)
Works to keep public lands accessible to bikers and provides information of trail design and maintenance. POB 7578, Boulder, CO 80306
(303) 545-9011, *www.greatoutdoors.com/imba*

National Off-Road Bicycling Association (NORBA)
National governing body of US mountain bike racing.
One Olympic Plaza, Colorado Springs, CO 80909
(719) 578-4717, *www.usacycling.org/mtb*

Outdoor Recreation Coalition of America (ORCA) Oversees and examines issues for outdoor recreation, Boulder, CO
(303) 444-3353, *www.orca.org*, *info@orca.org*

Rails-to-Trails Conservancy
Organized to promote conversion of abandoned rail corridors to trails for public use.
1400 16th Street, NW, Suite 300
Washington, D.C. 20036-2222, *www.railtrails.org*

League of American Wheelmen
190 West Ostend Street #120
Baltimore, MD 21230-3731
(410) 539-3399

United States Cycling Federation
Governing body for amateur cycling.
Colorado Springs, CO
(719) 578-4581, *www.usacycling.org*

USA Cycling
One Olympic Plaza
Colorado Springs, CO 80909
(719) 578-4581, *www.usacycling.org*

Boston Area:

Bicycle Coalition of Massachusetts
Cambridge, MA
www.massbike.org

Boston Brevet Services
Series of long distance, training and qualifying cycling events. Boston, MA
www.gisnet/~bbs

Charles River Wheelmen
Nonprofit, volunteer organization for the Greater Boston bicycling community for social riding. Not racing. West Newton, MA
www.crw.org

Middlesex Fells Mountain Bike Patrol
Cambridge, MA
www.ultranet.com/~kvk/nemba.html

Nashoba Valley Pedalers, Inc.
Bike club in Nashoba Valley area just west of Boston. Call for riding events and membership information package.
Acton, MA
(978) 266-1NVP
www.ultranet.com/~nvp/index.htm

New England Mountain Bike Patrol–Fells Patrol
1-800-57-NEMBA
www.nemba.org

North Shore Cyclists
Information on weekly and Sunday rides, clothing, and membership.
Wakefield, MA
www.astseals.com/nsc/welcome.html
mailing list: *nsc@cyclery.com*

Rage Mountain Bike Club
"Boston's coolest mountain bike club," quotes the website.
Cambridge, MA
www.rageMTB.com

Team Chuck
Mountain bike riders who enjoy fun rides in the Boston, MA area. North Quincy, MA
www.tiac.net/users/kca860/chuck1.htm

Tufts University Cycling Team
Medford, MA
mailing list: promoters@cyclery.com

Boston Area Racing Clubs

CCB
Racing team/club from the North Shore with year-round Saturday morning rides.
www1.shore.net/~tcm/ccb.html

Northeast Bicycle Club
One of the oldest racing clubs in the Boston area, welcoming racers of all abilities. Primarily a developmental club for new racers
http://world.std.com/~nebikclb/

Outside Boston area:

Fitchburg Cycling Club
North Central Massachusetts USCF/NORBA racing club. Sponsors of Longsjo Classic Stage Race
Ashby, MA
www.fitchburgcycling.org

MassBike
A comprehensive website for advocacy groups, racing groups, and other relevant event information. www.massbike.org

Narragansett Bay Wheelmen
Bicyling club serving riders in Rhode Island and Southeastern Massachusetts. Sponsor of "The Flattest Century in the East."
Tiverton, RI/MA www.nbwclub.org

New England Cycling Support Association
Supporting junior developmental and elite racers
Westport, MA
Marka Wise, Director, MarkaWI@aol.com

Seven Hills Wheelmen
Recreational group for adults of all riding abilities who also enjoy other outdoor activities
Worcester, MA
http://members.aol.com/shwworc/rides.htm

Ski Resorts

[...for mountain biking?]

Ski resorts offer a great alternative to local trail riding. During the spring, summer, and fall, many resorts will open their trails for mountain biking and, just like during ski season, sell lift tickets to take you and your bike to the top of the mountain. Lodging is also available for the weekend mountain bike junkies, and rates are often discounted from the normal ski-season prices. Some resorts will even rent bikes and lead guided mountain bike tours. Call ahead to find out just what each resort offers in the way of mountain bike riding, and pick the one that best suits your fancy.

The following is a list of many of the ski resorts near Boston that say *yes!* to mountain biking when the weather turns too warm for skiing.

Maine

Lost Valley
Auburn, ME
207-784-1561, *www.lostvalleyski.com*

Shawnee Peak
Bridgton, ME
(207) 647-8444 , *www.shawneepeak.com*

Sugarloaf/USA
Kingfield, ME
(207) 237-2000, *www.sugarloaf.com*

Sunday River
Bethel, ME
(207) 824-3000, *www.sundayriver.com*

Troll Valley Mountain Bike Park
West Farmington, ME
(207) 778-3656

New Hampshire

Attitash/Bear Peak
Bartlett, NH
(603) 374-2368, *www.attitash.com*

Bretton Woods
Bretton Woods, NH
(603) 278-3300, *www.brettonwoods.com*

Cannon Mountain
Franconia Notch, NH
(603) 823-5563 , *www.cannonmt.com*

Cranmore
North Conway, NH, (603) 356-5544

Franconia Village Cross-Country
Franconia, NH
1-800-473-5299, *www.franconiainn.com*

Loon Mountain Park
Lincoln, NH
(603) 745-8111, *www.loonmtn.com*

Mount Sunapee
Mount Sunapee, NH
(603) 763-2356, *www.mtsunapee.com*

Waterville Valley Mountain Bike Park
Waterville Valley, NH
1-800-468-2553, *www.waterville.com*

Wildcat
Pinkham Notch, Jackson, NH
1-888-4WILDCAT, *www.skiwildcat.com*

Fat Tire Vacations
[Bicycle Touring Companies]

There are literally dozens of off-road bicycling tour companies offering an incredible variety of guided tours for mountain bikers. On these pay-as-you-pedal, fat-tire vacations, you will have a chance to go places around the globe that only an expert can take you, and your experiences will be so much different than if seen through the window of a tour bus.

From Hut to Hut in the Colorado Rockies or Inn to Inn through Vermont's Green Mountains, there is a tour company for you. Whether you want hardcore singletrack during the day and camping at night, or you want scenic trails followed by a bottle of wine at night and a mint on each pillow, someone out there offers what you're looking for. The tours are well organized and fully supported with expert guides, bike mechanics, and "sag wagons" which carry gear, food, and tired bodies. Prices range from $100-$500 for a weekend to more than $2000 for two-week-long trips to far-off lands such as New Zealand or Ireland. Each of these companies will gladly send you their free literature to whet your appetite with breathtaking photography and titillating stories of each of their tours.

Selected Touring Companies

Maine
Backcountry Excursions
Limerick, ME, (207) 625-8189
www.wowpages.com/backcountry

New Hampshire
The Biking Expedition
(student cycling tours)
Henniker, NH, 1-800-245-4649
www.bikingx.com/index.html

Elk River Touring Center
Slatyfork, WV, (304) 572-3771

Vermont Bicycling Touring
Bristol, VT, 1-800-245-3868

Backroads
Berkley, CA, 1-800-BIKE TRIP

Timberline Bicycle Tours
Denver, CO, (303) 759-3804

Roads Less Traveled
Longmont, CO, (303) 678-8750

Blackwater Bikes
Davis, WV, (304) 259-5286

Bicycle Adventures
Olympia, WA, 1-800-443-6060

Trails Unlimited, Inc.
Nashville, IN, (812) 988-6232

Repair
and
Mainten

FIXING A FLAT

TOOLS YOU WILL NEED

- Two tire irons
- Pump (either a floor pump or a frame pump)
- No screwdrivers!!! (This can puncture the tube)

REMOVING THE WHEEL

The front wheel is easy. Simply open the quick release mechanism or undo the bolts with the proper sized wrench, then remove the wheel from the bike.

The rear wheel is a little more tricky. Before you loosen the wheel from the frame, shift the chain into the smallest gear on the freewheel (the cluster of gears in the back). Once you've done this, removing and installing the wheel, like the front, is much easier.

REMOVING THE TIRE

Step one: Insert a tire iron under the bead of the tire and pry the tire over the lip of the rim. Be careful not to pinch the tube when you do this.

Step two: Hold the first tire iron in place. With the second tire iron, repeat step one, three or four inches down the rim. Alternate tire irons, pulling the bead of the tire over the rim, section by section, until one side of the tire bead is completely off the rim.

Step three: Remove the rest of the tire and tube from the rim. This can be done by hand. It's easiest to remove the valve stem last. Once the tire is off the rim, pull the tube out of the tire.

CLEAN AND SAFETY CHECK

Step four: Using a rag, wipe the inside of the tire to clean out any dirt, sand, glass, thorns, etc. These may cause the tube to puncture. The inside of a tire should feel smooth. Any pricks or bumps could mean that you have found the culprit responsible for your flat tire.

Step five: Wipe the rim clean, then check the rim strip, making sure it covers the spoke nipples properly on the inside of the rim. If a spoke is poking through the rim strip, it could cause a puncture.

Step six: At this point, you can do one of two things: replace the punctured tube with a new one, or patch the hole. It's easiest to just replace the tube with a new tube when you're out on the trails. Roll up the old tube and take it home to repair later that night in front of the TV. Directions on patching a tube are usually included with the patch kit itself.

INSTALLING THE TIRE AND TUBE
(This can be done entirely by hand)

Step seven: Inflate the new or repaired tube with enough air to give it shape, then tuck it back into the tire.

Step eight: To put the tire and tube back on the rim, begin by putting the valve in the valve hole. The valve must be straight. Then use your hands to push the beaded edge of the tire onto the rim all the way around so that one side of your tire is on the rim.

Step nine: Let most of the air out of the tube to allow room for the rest of the tire.

Step ten: Beginning opposite the valve, use your thumbs to push the other side of the tire onto the rim. Be careful not to pinch the tube in between the tire and the rim. The last few inches may be difficult, and you may need the tire iron to pry the tire onto the rim. If so, just be careful not to puncture the tube.

BEFORE INFLATING COMPLETELY

Step eleven: Check to make sure the tire is seated properly and that the tube is not caught between the tire and the rim. Do this by adding about 5 to 10 pounds of air, and watch closely that the tube does not bulge out of the tire.

Step twelve: Once you're sure the tire and tube are properly seated, put the wheel back on the bike, then fill the tire with air. It's easier squeezing the wheel through the brake shoes if the tire is still flat.

Step thirteen: Now fill the tire with the proper amount of air, and check constantly to make sure the tube doesn't bulge from the rim. If the tube does appear to bulge out, release all the air as quickly as possible, or you could be in for a big bang.

• When installing the rear wheel, place the chain back onto the smallest cog (furthest gear on the right), and pull the derailleur out of the way. Your wheel should slide right on.

LUBRICATION PREVENTS DETERIORATION

Lubrication is crucial to maintaining your bike. Dry spots will be eliminated. Creaks, squeaks, grinding, and binding will be gone. The chain will run quietly, and the gears will shift smoothly. The brakes will grip quicker, and your bike may last longer with fewer repairs. Need I say more? Well, yes. Without knowing where to put the lubrication, what good is it?

THINGS YOU WILL NEED
• One can of bicycle lubricant, found at any bike store.
• A clean rag (to wipe excess lubricant away).

WHAT GETS LUBRICATED
• Front derailleur
• Rear derailleur
• Shift levers
• Front brake
• Rear brake

- Both brake levers
- Chain

WHERE TO LUBRICATE

To make it easy, simply spray a little lubricant on all the pivot points of your bike. If you're using a squeeze bottle, use just a drop or two. Put a few drops on each point wherever metal moves against metal, for instance, at the center of the brake calipers. Then let the lube sink in.

Once you have applied the lubricant to the derailleurs, shift the gears a few times, working the derailleurs back and forth. This allows the lubricant to work itself into the tiny cracks and spaces it must occupy to do its job. Work the brakes a few times as well.

LUBING THE CHAIN

Lubricating the chain should be done after the chain has been wiped clean of most road grime. Do this by spinning the pedals counterclockwise while gripping the chain with a clean rag. As you add the lubricant, be sure to get some in between each link. With an aerosol spray, just spray the chain while pedalling backwards (counterclockwise) until the chain is fully lubricated. Let the lubricant soak in for a few seconds before wiping the excess away. Chains will collect dirt much faster if they're loaded with too much lubrication.

Index

Euphoria...
in many different states.

The most beautiful, challenging and exhilarating rides are just a day-trip away.

Visit **www.outside-america.com** to order the latest guides for areas near you – or not so near. Also, get information and updates on future publications and other guidebooks from Outside America™.

For more information or to place an order, Call **1-800-243-0495.**

OUTSIDE AMERICA GUIDES

Mountain Bike
AMERICA™

Meet the Author

Jeff fell in love with the sport of mountain biking in early 1995 when he spent time attacking the trails on a modified hybrid. Later that year, his grandmother gave him a "real" mountain bike and opened the door to harsher trails, longer rides, and numerous memories. Jeff has since participated in dual slalom at Mount Snow, cross-country time trials in Massachusetts, and a mountain bike visit to Ireland for the 1998 Tour de France (he didn't race). As a writer, Jeff has worked for a variety of organizations and publications including Reebok, Ford Motor Company, *Dirt Rag*, *Mountain Biking*, and *SingleTracks Magazine*.